A REFERENCE PUBLICATION IN LITERATURE

Ronald Gottesman, *Editor*

John Barth, Jerzy Kosinski, and Thomas Pynchon:
A Reference Guide

Thomas P. Walsh
Cameron Northouse

G. K. HALL & CO., 70 LINCOLN STREET, BOSTON, MASS.

Copyright © 1977 by Thomas P. Walsh and Cameron Northouse

Library of Congress Cataloging in Publication Data

Walsh, Thomas P
     John Barth, Jerzy Kosinski, and Thomas Pynchon.

     (A Reference publication in literature)
     Includes indexes.
     1. American fiction--20th century--Bibliography.
2. Barth, John--Bibliography. 3. Kosinski, Jerzy N.,
1933-   --Bibliography. 4. Pynchon, Thomas--
Bibliography. I. Northouse, Cameron, joint author.
II. Title. III. Series.
Z1231.F4W34   [PS379]   016.813'5'4   77-10918
ISBN 0-8161-7910-7

This publication is printed on permanent/durable acid-free paper
MANUFACTURED IN THE UNITED STATES OF AMERICA

Contents

Introduction

As satirists, John Barth, Jerzy Kosinski, and Thomas Pynchon use many similar techniques in their fictional inquiries into the dilemmas of modern men and women in conflict with themselves and their world. These writers can laugh at their characters and the society that produces them, but they also maintain the serious side of the ironic tradition of Swift and Voltaire. This is a remedial tradition that requires that the satirist correct human folly and error, that the scalpel-wielding, ironic anatomist may flay his creations for their foibles, but he must also draw attention to correct modes of behavior and serious views of life, thought, and art. Barth, Kosinski, and Pynchon hold up an often shocking mirror to the faults of human nature, and they allow us to see ourselves for what we all too often are.

Perhaps here the comparison should end because these writers project very different visions of the world, and their writing styles vividly contrast. For example, since the beginning of his career, John Barth has been criticized for breaking middle-class taboos and using salacious language. Barth, born May 27, 1930, is the oldest of these writers. Well educated, holding an A.B. and M.A., both from Johns Hopkins University, Barth has maintained a close affiliation with higher education through his sojourns with Pennsylvania State University and the State University of New York at Buffalo as a teacher and writer in residence. There is a definite academic orientation in his works (culminating in Goat-Boy); even early reviewers called him a writer concerned with ideas and ideology.

Although Barth has always been taken seriously, reviewers and critics have continued to comment on his comic talents, praising, for example, The Sot-Weed Factor for its hilarious episodes as well as for its authentically witty restoration language. The Floating Opera and The End of the Road had marked Barth as a pessimist and existentialist, even a nihilist (which Barth readily acknowledges), but The Sot-Weed Factor—even though it too received outcries of disgust and distaste at its candor, ribaldry, and frank language—turned reviewers and critics toward Barth's talents as an Absurdist. The publication of Giles Goat-Boy confirmed this evaluation because reviewers

acclaimed it as a very literary novel, an elaborate conceit, and they
praised its incorporation of allegory and myth.

By 1967 critics were naturally beginning to make comparisons and
contrasts among and between the works. Many felt The Sot-Weed Factor
was superior to Giles Goat-Boy, although both novels received adverse
criticism because of their "excessive" detail and wordiness. Now
Barth came to be known as one of the more intellectual of the American Black Humorists. The cerebral and metaphysical qualities of Lost
in the Funhouse (1968) fleshed out this image and led commentators to
make more extensive analyses of Barth's works. There were those who
complained of confusion in Barth's fiction, but most critics praised
Barth for allegorical, imagistic, mythic narratives and deep, rich
prose. They began to look back at The End of the Road, particularly
in their comparisons with Lost in the Funhouse, and deeper analyses
of all Barth's works drew forth more favorable considerations of the
earlier novels.

So, in the early seventies, many longer studies of Barth's alle-
gorizing and myth-making appeared. Most were favorable, but questioned Barth's sense of humor and lack of character growth in his
novels. Such criticism appeared at the same time that most commentators labeled him as a Black Humorist.

Upon the publication of Chimera, many reviewers remarked on what
Barth himself has stated is a recurrent problem in his works: as he
puts it, "the discrepancy between art and the Real Thing. . . ."
Barth says that one way to come to terms with this is "to affirm the
artificial element in art . . . and make the artifice part of your
point. . . ." Often the result of Barth's affirmation has been the
inclusion of large chunks of erudite material, philosophizing. Many
reviewers have found these rather indigestible; others have continued
to object to "raw sex" in his novels. Chimera has particularly called
forth comments on Barth's use of classical sources. Barth's typical
answer to much of this criticism has been that he likes to make
simple things complicated.

Finally, the most recent readers of Barth have turned toward
studies of his themes. In these and in respect to his style, they
have frequently noted Barth's debt to James Joyce. The longer
studies of Barth's canon have begun to stress the author's attention
to modern American problems of identity, Barth's parodic style, his
baroque treatment. Chimera has continued to receive high praise.

Jerzy Kosinski's more recent works have also focused on modern
American problems, but this was not always the case. Kosinski was
born in Poland on June 14, 1933; he grew up there. He did not emi-
grate to the United States until 1957, at which time he mastered the
English language. Kosinski also has an intense academic background
and concentration: he holds two degrees from the University of Lodz
(Poland) and was a Ph.D. candidate in sociology at Columbia University

for some years; he also attended the New School for Social Research
for two years. Since the success of his later novels, he has become
less active in academic pursuits.

Kosinski did not, however, begin as a novelist; his first two
books were reportorial essays on first-hand impressions of Russian
life, written under the pseudonym of Joseph Novak. The Future is
Ours, Comrade and No Third Path were published in 1960 and received
favorably by most reviewers as candid and informative observations
of the Russians. Although many reviewers praised Kosinski's descrip-
tions for their realism, others cast some doubt on the authenticity
of the interviews recorded by Kosinski. Whereas some commentators
praised Kosinski's "insider's" point of view, others asked why he
couldn't be more analytical. There was general agreement that the
interviews were the most interesting parts of the books.

Kosinski's first novel, The Painted Bird, received immediate ac-
claim for its "autobiographical truth," its shocking episodes. There
was also immediate interest in its structural meaning, its symbolic
mode, and its folktale qualities. Most reviewers were taken with the
novel's power, but many questioned its morality. Because Kosinski
had written two earlier books which purported to be based on real interviews and observations, some reviewers treated The Painted Bird as
if it were a document and not a novel. This is certainly a tribute
to Kosinski's stark realism, but an oddity nevertheless. In the year
following its publication, the inevitable critical comparisons of
The Painted Bird started, and critics attempted to classify the novel,
particularly in terms of its visual prose and mythic qualities. It
seemed inevitable also that The Painted Bird would be condemned in
Poland because of its harsh picture of bureaucratic and peasant behavior in Polish territory during and after the Second World War.
When The Painted Bird went into a paperback edition, much was made of
the omission of what critics called "Joseph Novak's intrusion," the
political sermon that had been tacked on the end of the novel.

Steps, Kosinski's second novel, was seen by some as the conse-
quential production of one who had lived the life of the young pro-
tagonist in The Painted Bird. But the laudatory structural criticism
that marked the reviews of The Painted Bird were missing; most ob-
jected to Steps on the grounds that it was a disconnected effort,
lacking the substance also of the former effort. Now, however, reviewers began to recognize Kosinski's European roots in Sartrean
existentialism. They praised the novel for its attention to evil,
even though they caviled that the novel did not serve as much of a
moral study. There were those, however, who believed Steps a better
novel than The Painted Bird, those who especially praised the devices
of narration. Kafka became the inevitable comparison, and puzzlement
and praise could be found in almost all reviews and criticisms. Such
criticisms were not always laudatory; often comparison of Kosinski
with Kafka became a means of belittling Kosinski, a way of finding
shortcomings in Kosinski's works.

Steps was also adversely reviewed for its coldness (narrative treatment) and sex (incidental). Some reviewers found the indifference and detachment of the narrator nugatory; they believed too much was being asked of the reader. The complaints about sexuality were the usual ones attending to Kosinski's productions: many felt the sexual incidents were not normal expressions of human sexuality, but were "kinky" and sensational manifestations of human degradation. By 1970 Kosinski was defending his philosophy and art by replying that the human sin he depicted can be "any act which prevents the self from functioning freely." Society and religion, Kosinski opines, are too often the sources of such sin.

Longer studies of Kosinski's art began to place him with Barth as a satirist, but they stressed Kosinski's unique vision, different from Barth and others because in Kosinski's works ideas are as important as physical sensations. The publication of Being There marked the emergence of Kosinski as a humorist. Some praised this aspect of his novel as very original, while others found it too obvious. Many reviewers admired the style and thought of Being There, but others saw it as a degeneration and wondered at its elusive moral. Adverse criticism noted the "soap opera" dialogue and lack of realism in Being There, but still praised its ironic tone.

By 1972 Kosinski was being seen as one of the Black Humorists. Reviewers were puzzled by the fragmented form and people of The Devil Tree, but commentators felt Kosinski's new novel followed his usual philosophical approach. Longer studies of Kosinski's works focused on his portrayal of violence and his imagistic style, dwelling particularly on Kosinski's continued questioning of freedom and existence. Those not taken with The Devil Tree called the author an "abstractionist" writing "depression literature." Perhaps the most interesting indictment against Kosinski was the charge of commercialism. He had become very popular, a type of success not easily forgiven by some serious reviewers of "literature."

Unlike Kosinski, Thomas Pynchon has deep roots in American history and culture. The first Pynchon arrived in the new world in 1630 and became treasurer of the Massachusetts Bay Colony. Thomas Pynchon, born May 8, 1937, in Long Island, has used his family's history as a source for characterization in his novels, particularly in Gravity's Rainbow. The Pynchons have produced many prominent Americans, but perhaps few who were as shy as Thomas, a notable recluse who, it is said, does not even allow his picture to be shown on the jackets of his novels.

Although his career as a novelist is a distinguished one, Thomas Pynchon has preferred to remain in the background. This was true even when he was a student at Cornell University, from which he graduated with honors in 1958, but where few remember him. Nevertheless, with the publication of V in 1963, Pynchon began to receive a good deal of attention. Many of his reviewers were frankly puzzled: was

INTRODUCTION

$\underline{V}$ a satire or a romance; was it even to be considered as a work of
art? Those who were not puzzled called the novel boring and/or nihilistic and left it at that, but those who responded to $\underline{V}$ on the
deepest levels labelled it the "new picaresque." They lauded Pynchon's irony and choice of words; they compared him with Sterne and
West. All agreed that Pynchon's novel was complex and noted his
ability as a careful researcher.

The farce and comedy of $\underline{V}$ appealed to many, who placed Pynchon
among the larger group of American pessimistic writers, creators of
anti-heroes. The William Faulkner Foundation provided Pynchon its
First Novel Award. Now Pynchon was recognized more readily as a member of America's nihilistic Black Humorist group, but he was being
seen as a serious social critic as well. Comparisons to Barth and
others stressed, however, Pynchon's talent for writing absurd fiction, critical socially because it portrayed the "anti-face" of the
American dream. Barth, himself, denied that he and Pynchon were
trying to do the same thing.

Pynchon's second novel, The Crying of Lot 49, published in 1966,
drew criticism similar to that which attended $\underline{V}$'s reviews. Some ob-
jected to the second novel, calling it a hoax, yawning in boredom,
being incensed at its hyperbolic language; The Crying of Lot 49 was
damned almost immediately as a "Slapstick Novel," an absurd novel of
the absurd. But those reviewers who connected Lot 49 with $\underline{V}$ searched
for lines of development from one novel to the other. Some felt that
Lot 49 was an even more imaginative creation than $\underline{V}$; it, too, was
full of despair and the absurd. In this sense it received comparisons
with The Great Gatsby. These labels stuck through 1967 and 1968 as
classification of Pynchon as a Black Humorist became more certain.
But more and more critics began to analyze Pynchon's technique,
praising him for his psychic penetration and his energy, damning him
for problems of narration and for lack of character motivation,
recognizing him as a self-parodist.

By 1969 and 1970 many commentators were emphasizing the quality
of Pynchon's complex plotting. Some insisted that Barth had heavily
influenced the younger novelist. Others, however, pointed to the im-
pact of our scientific culture on Pynchon's imagination, citing the
novelist's thematic use of the Quantum theory and Entropy. These,
they indicated, provided the backdrop for the motif of dream and illusion in the novels. Pynchon's critics in the early 1970's focused,
therefore, on the novelist's depiction of isolated characters faced
with the death of the American dream. Again Pynchon was compared to
Barth as another writer creating a disordered world, a "humorous
apocalypse."

Gravity's Rainbow, published in 1973, received the kind of mixed
reaction from reviewers that had been accorded the first two novels.
It was called eccentric, excessive, demanding--and too cute! Many
found Pynchon's narrative a "dizzying" experience, absurd in itself.

Introduction

But more lengthy analyses of Pynchon's works bordered on the enthusiastic, especially those which centered on Pynchon's philosophical approach. Pynchon's works showed us the "irrational world of objects." Here was a world filled with paranoia, complexly invented and sometimes described in a stylistically abstruse manner, but a world nevertheless created by a writer seriously concerned with our present cultural predicaments. In this world were characters who attempted to provide themselves, at least, with illusory concepts of reality. Here again Pynchon was compared favorably with Barth. Most unfavorable comments on Pynchon's art focused on deficiencies of characterization, faults in basic techniques of creation. These have, however, been fewer and fewer by the mid-1970's. Gravity's Rainbow has recently been favorably compared with Thomas Mann's The Magic Mountain and James Joyce's Ulysses, high praise indeed.

This Reference Guide to John Barth, Jerzy Kosinski, and Thomas Pynchon is divided into three sections, one on each writer. Each section has the same structure and intent. The first part lists their works, in chronological order of publication. The second part records the major writings we have found about them, again in chronological order of publication. Arrangement within each year is alphabetical by author. All entries are annotated with a brief abstract of the content of the work. We have tried to be comprehensive in our annotations. There are separate indexes to each part of this book.

ACKNOWLEDGMENTS

We wish to express our appreciation for all the valuable help we have received in the researching and writing of this guide. First, we wish to thank Audrey Wickhiser for her research assistance and typing skills, and Mrs. Valerie Shubik for research assistance. Also, we wish to thank the University of Nebraska at Omaha for support from the University Senate Research Committee and the Inter-library Loan Department. Without them, the completion of this project would not have been possible.

John Barth

Writings by John Barth

Books

The Floating Opera. New York: Appleton-Century-Crofts, 1956.
Toronto: S. J. R. Saunders, 1956. New York: Avon Books
(Avon Library), 1965.

The Floating Opera. (Rev. Ed.) Garden City, N. Y.: Doubleday &
Co., 1967. Toronto: Doubleday, Canada, 1967. London:
Secker & Warburg, 1968. Harmondsworth, Middlesex: Penguin
Books, 1970.

The End of the Road. Garden City, N. Y.: Doubleday & Co.,
1958. Toronto: Doubleday, Canada, 1958. New York: Avon
Books, 1960. London: Secker & Warburg, 1962. London:
Brown & Watson, 1964. New York: Avon Books (Avon Library),
1964.

The End of the Road. (Rev. Ed.) Garden City, N. Y.:
Doubleday & Co., 1967. Harmondsworth, Middlesex: Penguin
Books, 1967. Toronto: Doubleday, Canada, 1967. New York:
Bantam Books, 1969. New York: Grosset & Dunlap (Universal
Library), 1969.

The Sot-Weed Factor. Garden City, N. Y.: Doubleday & Co., 1960.
Toronto: Doubleday, Canada, 1960. London: Secker &
Warburg, 1961. New York: Grosset & Dunlap (Universal
Library), 1964. Toronto: George J. McLeod, 1964. London:
Panther Books, 1965. New York: Grosset & Dunlap (Grosset
Specials), 1966.

The Sot-Weed Factor. (Rev. Ed.) Garden City, N. Y.: Doubleday &
Co., 1967. Toronto: Doubleday, Canada, 1967. New York:
Bantam Books, 1969.

Giles Goat-Boy; or, The Revised New Syllabus. Garden City,
N. Y.: Doubleday & Co., 1966. Garden City, N. Y.:
Doubleday & Co., 1966 (limited edition: numbered, signed).

Greenwich, Conn.: Fawcett, 1967. London: Secker &
Warburg, 1967. Harmondsworth, Middlesex: Penguin Books,
1968.

Lost in the Funhouse; Fiction for Print, Tape, Live Voice.
Garden City, N. Y.: Doubleday & Co., 1968. Garden City,
N. Y.: Doubleday & Co., 1968 (limited edition: numbered,
signed). Toronto: Doubleday, Canada, 1968. London:
Secker & Warburg, 1969. New York: Bantam Books, 1969.
New York: Grosset & Dunlap (Universal Library), 1969.

Chimera. New York: Random House, 1972. New York: Fawcett
World, 1973.

Short Fiction

"Lilith and the Lion." The Hopkins Review, 4 (Fall 1950),
49-53.

"The Remobilization of Jacob Horner." Esquire, 50 (July 1958),
55-59.

"Landscape, The Eastern Shore." Kenyon Review, 22 (Winter 1960),
104-110.

"Water-Message." Southwest Review, 48 (1963), 226-237.

"Ambrose His Mark." Esquire, 59 (Fall 1963), 97, 122-124,
126-127.

"Test Borings." In Modern Occasions. Edited by Philip Rahes.
New York: Garrar, Straus and Giroux, 1966, pp. 247-263.

"Night-Sea Journey." Esquire, 65 (June 1966), 82-83, 147-148.

"Lost in the Funhouse." Atlantic, 220 (November 1967), 73-82.

"Petition: Story." Esquire, 70 (July 1968), 68-71, 135.

"Title." Yale Review, 47 (Winter 1968), 213-221.

"Autobiography: A Self-Recorded Fiction." New American Review,
2 (1968), 72-75.

"Help: A Stereophonic Narrative for Authorial Voice." Esquire,
72 (September 1969), 108-109.

"Dunyazadiad." Esquire, 77 (June 1972), 136-142.

"Perseid." Harpers, 245 (September 1972), 79-96.

Writings by John Barth

Non-Fiction

"My Two Muses." The John Hopkins Magazine, 12 (April 1961),
    9-13.

"Afterward." In The Adventures of Roderick Random by Tobias
    Smollett. New York: The New American Library, 1964,
    pp. 469-479.

"Muse, Spare Me." Book Week, 26 September 1965, pp. 28-29.

"A Gift of Books." Holiday, 40 (December 1966), 171.

"Literature of Exhaustion." Atlantic Monthly, 220 (August 1967),
    29-34.

"Censorship--1967: A Series of Symposia." Arts in Society, 4
    (1967), 265-358.

"A Tribute to Vladimir Nabokov." In Nabokov: Criticism,
    Reminiscences, Translations and Tributes. Edited by Alfred
    Appel, Jr. and Charles Newman. Evanston: Northwestern
    University Press, 1970, p. 350.

"A Tribute to John Hawkes." The Harvard Advocate, 104
    (October 1970), 11.

Writings about
John Barth, 1956-1973

1956

1 ADELMAN, GEORGE. Review of The Floating Opera. Library
   Journal, 81 (August), 1789.
      Summary of plot. Something of Celine, Camus and Sterne
   but not all successful. Entertaining first novel.

2 ANON. Review of The Floating Opera. Los Angeles Mirror and
   Daily News, 20 August, II, p. 2.
      Novel not for your "prissy Aunt Minnie." Characters'
   curiosity about life similar to "Tris Shandy, Candide and
   Mark Twain in his off moments."

3 ANON. "First Novel Inspired by Famous Showboat." Springfield
   Sunday Republican, 12 August, Sec. C, p. 12.
      Review of The Floating Opera. Points out Barth con-
   ceived idea of novel when he saw showboat photo by Boding.
   Reminded him of one docked in home town of Cambridge, Md.

4 COOPER, MADISON. "Chockfull of Curiosities." Dallas Morning
   News, 14 October, Part 5, p. 15.
      Review of The Floating Opera. Needs credulity to sus-
   tain interest. Barth appears to have listed taboos not
   seen in previously written works and tries to see how many
   he can get away with.

5 GOLWYN, J. "New Creative Writers." Library Journal, 81
   (June), 1496-1497.
      Short biography of Barth and a synopsis of The Floating
   Opera.

6 HARDING, W. "Needless Vulgarity in Novel." Chicago Sunday
   Tribune, 21 October, p. 14.
      Review of The Floating Opera. Strangely constructed but
   fascinatingly unique. Barth's vulgarity adds nothing to
   understanding of characters.

1956

7 _____. Review of The Floating Opera. Kirkus, 24 (15 June),
417.
Sketch of plot, calls novel "a deliberately digressive
and . . . smugly salacious report on the life and times
of Todd Andrews. . . ."

8 HOGAN, WILLIAM. "Life is a Showboat, a Young Author Finds."
San Francisco Chronicle, 28 August, p. 19.
Review of The Floating Opera. Barth has "disarming
screwball talent." Novel heavy in symbolism. Author is
closer to "experimental writing of the little magazine
than to a novel of general interest." Would like to see
what Barth does at age 36.

9 MANDEL, S. "Gaudy Showboat." New York Times, 26 August,
p. 27.
Review of The Floating Opera. Novel goes straight for
the jugular. Point is that it's better to choose among
relative values than to reject all by suicide. Barth puts
new life in old genre.

10 MYERS, ART. "Life's but a Showboat Drifting By." Washington
Post and Times Herald, 26 August, p. E6.
Review of The Floating Opera. Structure unpredictable
and stimulating. Except for the "turgid" ending, the novel
is a delight.

11 PRESCOTT, ORVILLE. "Books of the Times." New York Times,
3 September, p. 11.
Review of The Floating Opera. Not funny enough to make
up for faults which include dullness, labored humor and
cheap attempts to shock.

12 RUBIN, LOUIS D., JR. "Novel of the Eastern Shore and War."
Baltimore Evening Sun, 27 August, p. 16.
Review of The Floating Opera. Comic work with sober
overtones. Barth appears to be preoccupied with the form,
but the fiction is still successful.

13 SCHICKEL, RICHARD. "An 'Opera' Afloat." Milwaukee Journal,
30 December, p. 4.
Review of The Floating Opera. "Highly original comic
novel with philosophical overtones or as a philosophical
novel with comic overtones." A delightful product of a
first-class mind.

WRITINGS ABOUT JOHN BARTH, 1956-1973

1957

1   ANON. "Comic Opera." <u>Omaha World Herald</u>, 13 January,
       Sec. C, p. 29.
           Review of <u>The Floating Opera</u>. Hilarity never lets up.
       "Very funny novel."

1958

1   ANON. Review of <u>End of the Road</u>. <u>Kirkus</u>, 26 (15 May), 362.
           Rehash of plot. Book is representative of type by
       Kerouac and Herbert Gold. For those "schooled in the
       waste matter of the body and the mind; for others, a real
       recoil."

2   ANON. Review of <u>End of the Road</u>. <u>Library Journal</u>, 83
       (1 September), 2319.
           Plot sounds absurd but asks questions about choice and
       the meaning of life. Writing is very good, but may shock
       some readers.

3   ANON. Review of <u>End of the Road</u>. <u>Time</u> (21 July), p. 80.
           Mentions <u>The Floating Opera</u>. Summary of plot. Barth
       has good ear for "psychologizing claptrap" that is used
       for conversation in some circles. Has produced that rarity,
       a true novel of ideas.

4   LAHAYE, JUDSON. Review of <u>End of the Road</u>. <u>Best Sellers</u>, 18
       (1 August), 165.
           Novel's insistence on "I don't know" as solution for
       his characters' problems produces only quality of despair
       in spite of writing excellence. Extraordinary in talent
       but neither "moral nor human."

5   WERMUTH, PAUL C. Review of <u>End of the Road</u>. <u>Library Journal</u>,
       23 (1 September), 2319-2320.
           Novel is interesting, witty but some puzzling questions
       raised concerning the role of choice and meaning in life.

1959

1   KERNER, DAVID. "Psychodrama in Eden." <u>Chicago Review</u>, 13
       (Winter/Spring), 59-67.
           Analysis of <u>End of the Road</u>. Mentions <u>The Floating
       Opera</u>. Characters dispute human nature. Self pitted
       against non-self, real against vacuum, etc. Contests

1960

suggest medieval allegory. Book is pretentious in showing
nihilism as a product of thought. Intention is excellent,
to blend "novel, ideology, allegory, psychodrama and farce."

<u>1960</u>

1   ANON. Review of <u>The Sot-Weed Factor</u>. <u>Kirkus</u>, 28 (15 June),
      462.
          Plot complex but clear, poetically displays manners,
      morals and language of the period. Also finds prominent
      incidents of disgust and distaste as in <u>End of the Road</u>.

2   ANON. "I' Faith, 'Tis Good." <u>Newsweek</u>, 54 (29 August), 88-89.
          Review of <u>The Sot-Weed Factor</u>. Summary of plot. Serious
      point does emerge from the "wild vagaries and characters."

3   ANON. "The Virgin Laureate." <u>Time</u> (5 September), p. 77.
          Review of <u>The Sot-Weed Factor</u>. Summary of plot. Novel
      is bawdy and ironic. It is "a genuinely serious comedy."

4   BARKER, SHIRLEY. "History is Still Good Fiction." <u>Saturday</u>
      <u>Review</u> (26 November), p. 21.
          Review of <u>The Sot-Weed Factor</u>. Imagination, skill and
      humor but one must have a strong stomach. Summary of plot.

5   BLUESTONE, GEORGE. "John Wain and John Barth. The Angry and
      the Accurate." <u>Massachusetts Review</u>, 1 (Summer), 582-589.
          Comparison of Wain and Barth with Barth coming off the
      better of the two. Mentions <u>The Floating Opera</u> and <u>End of</u>
      <u>the Road</u>. Barth is more honest and more accurate in con-
      fronting our situation. Examines the inadequacy of language
      to express the inexpressable. Barth seen as a genuine rebel
      with Wain a tired counterfeit.

6   FIEDLER, LESLIE A. <u>Love and Death in the American Novel</u>.
      New York: Criterion Books, p. 471.
          Mentions John Barth of <u>The Floating Opera</u> as the author
      most often suggesting the deepest truth about our existence.
      That it is absurd.

7   FULLER, EDMUND. "The Joke is on Mankind." <u>New York Times</u>
      <u>Book Review</u>, 21 August, p. 4.
          Review of <u>The Sot-Weed Factor</u>. Mentions <u>End of the Road</u>
      and <u>The Floating Opera</u>. Brilliant specialized performance.
      Plot is a parody of complexity. A book to be cherished by
      its true audience.

8   HARDING, WALTER. "An Historical Novel to End All Historical
      Novels." Chicago Sunday Tribune, 21 August, p. 5.
          Review of The Sot-Weed Factor. Hilariously complex and
      confusing. Novel can be read on many levels: deadpan,
      satire or as novel in the great eighteenth century
      tradition.

9   McLAUGHLIN, RICHARD. Review of The Sot-Weed Factor.
      Springfield Republican, 25 September, p. 4D.
          Finds a real seriousness at the bottom of the "racy
      comic" adventures. Gives summary of the plot.

10 ROBIE, B. A. Review of The Sot-Weed Factor. Library Journal,
      85 (15 September), 3099.
          Recommended. "Written in true spirit and language of
      the restoration period." A large slice of human comedy.

11 SOUTHERN, TERRY. "New Trends and Old Hats." Nation
      (19 November), pp. 380-383.
          Review of The Sot-Weed Factor. Mentions The End of the
      Road. Book's destructive function includes its tediousness,
      length, and price. It is more of a literary event than a
      novel.

12 WALSH, WILLIAM J., S.J. Review of The Sot-Weed Factor. Best
      Sellers, 20 (15 September), 200-201.
          Barth writes with "lucidity and verve," but his range of
      interests and effects are specialized so as to limit his
      audience to mature readers whose sensibilities are not
      shaken by "Rabelaisian approach to man's folly."

1961

1   ANON. "Invitation to Escape." Times Literary Supplement
      (27 October), p. 765.
          Review of The Sot-Weed Factor. Hard to tell how seri-
      ously Barth wants to be taken. We expect our historical
      novels to show awareness of "psychology, motive and social
      development." Barth's does not.

2   KING, FRANCIS. "Smog of the Spirit." New Statesman
      (13 October), p. 524.
          Review of The Sot-Weed Factor. "Brilliant pastiche of
      late seventeenth and early eighteenth century literature."
      Enjoyable but its appeal is apt to be specialized.

1961

3 SUTCLIFFE, DENHAM. "Worth a Guilty Conscience." The Kenyon
   Review, 23:181-184.
        Review of The Sot-Weed Factor. Picaresque, which is
   also a burlesque of historical novels. Style is one of
   "untiring exuberance, limitless fertility of imagination
   . . . a breathless pace of narrative. . . ."

                            1962

1 ANON. "Fiction by Tyndareus." John O'London's, 7
   (27 September), 4.
        Brief review of End of the Road. Plot summary. Charac-
   terized as a hard to define novel where tragedy and comedy
   are mixed.

2 ANON. "Strife and Struggle." Times Literary Supplement
   (28 September), p. 757.
        Review of The End of the Road. Mentions The Sot-Weed
   Factor. Interesting developments fade into a dull mire of
   repetition. The anti-hero is an all too familiar creation.

3 BRADBURY, M. "New Novels." Punch (10 October), p. 540.
        Review of End of the Road. An amusing, profound novel
   but too imitative and unsure. Still of high quality. A
   philosophical novel in high comedy style.

4 COLEMAN, JOHN. Review of The End of the Road. The Queen
   (London), 221 (18 September), 27-28.
        Novel starts as shrewd and funny, but progresses finally
   as hard and crude. Becomes a genuinely moving inquiry into
   marital acquaintanceship. Although the end is in blood and
   dust, the previous arguments have been worthier.

5 ETHRIDGE, JAMES M., ed. "John Barth." In Contemporary
   Authors: The International Bio-Bibliographical Guide to
   Current Authors and Their Works. Detroit: Gale Research
   Co., p. 24.
        Short biography of Barth and a bibliography of his works.

6 HASSAN, IHAB. "The Existential Novel." The Massachusetts
   Review, 3 (Summer), 795-797.
        Hassan sets forth and illustrates three basic proposi-
   tions which apply to the existential novel: 1) The world
   of the existential novel is basically void of presupposi-
   tions; 2) the hero's purpose is to create meaning out of
   the meaningless; and 3) the form is ironic "low mimetic

mode." Barth's hero in <u>End of the Road</u> is one of the il-
lustrations used for the second assertion.

7 RAVEN, SIMON. "A Lemon for the Teacher." <u>Spectator</u>
   (21 September), p. 410.
      Review of <u>End of the Road</u>. Study in the problems of
   identity and choice. Gets high marks as a novel of ideas.
   "Statement of classical pessimism."

8 RICHARDSON, MAURICE. "Upper Crusts." <u>New Statesman</u>
   (21 September), p. 370.
      Review of <u>End of the Road</u>. A disappointment after <u>The
   Sot-Weed Factor</u>. Barth can't quite manage "an effect of
   snarling tragic-farce."

1963

1 BRYER, JACKSON R. "Two Bibliographies." <u>Critique</u>, 6 (Fall),
   86-94.
      Comprehensive bibliography of Barth's work.

2 ROVIT, EARL. "The Novel as Parody: John Barth." <u>Critique</u>,
   6 (Fall), 77-85.
      Mentions <u>The Floating Opera</u>, but analyzes <u>The Sot-Weed
   Factor</u>. Sees novel as "a kind of prolonged academic joke."
   The author finds nothing of intrinsic merit, the novel produces "a shallow parody, an intellectual gymnastic, a me-
   chanical puzzle. . . ." This is accomplished through the
   parody of picaresque structure and "the main themes of
   18th-Century fiction." But there are "excessive parapher-
   nalia of authentic antiquarianism" smothering the parodic
   form. Claims Barth "meant to use a parody-form in order
   to make a more positive statement of the possibility of
   value. . . ."

3 SCHICKEL, RICHARD. "<u>The Floating Opera</u>." <u>Critique</u>, 6
   (Fall), 53-67.
      Schickel calls <u>Opera</u> the first of the novels produced by
   the "school" of comic novelists. Book is distinguished
   from works in this genre in that its hero is not neat and
   lifeless. He is not bored or boring as many existential
   heroes are. Novel also avoids the sameness of tone preva-
   lent in existential works. Schickel then goes through the
   hero's five experiences of intense emotion. Only criticism
   is that Barth does not fully explain the psychology of his
   characters. But the flaws are more than compensated for by

1963

its "many mature excellences." Opera is an essentially
philosophical novel that is alive.

4   SMITH, HERBERT F. "Barth's Endless Road." Critique, 6
    (Fall), 68–76.
        Mentions The Floating Opera and The Sot-Weed Factor.
    Analyzes End of the Road. Studies the allegorical aspects
    of the main characters and their relationship to the ni-
    hilistic themes. Demonstrates that a polarity develops be-
    tween "moral nihilism" and "ethical positivism." Believes
    this novel "is Barth's most bitter commentary to date on
    the plight of man."

5   TRACHTENBERG, ALLAN. "Barth and Hawkes: Two Fabulists."
    Critique, 6 (Fall), 4–18.
        Comparing Barth and Hawkes, Trachtenberg sees them as
    fabulists for whom traditionalism and realism are worn out.
    Hawke's fables give form to the implausibility of life.
    Barth's are intellectual positions embodied in character
    and action. Barth's novels are not allegories; there is
    enough realism for the reader to recognize common human be-
    havior. The Floating Opera, End of the Road and The Sot-
    Weed Factor mentioned as three works which are based on
    "cosmopsis." That is, the modern dilemma is forced when
    one recognizes the relativity of values and actions. Opera
    introduces this theme, End of the Road sharpens and clari-
    fies it, and The Sot-Weed Factor develops its implications.

1964

1   FIEDLER, LESLIE A. "The War Against the Academy." Wisconsin
    Studies in Contemporary Literature, 5:5–17. Also in
    Waiting for the End. New York: Stein and Day, pp. 153–154.
        Fiedler discusses the novelists who have found protec-
    tion and employment in the university setting. He says of
    Barth that with the publication of The Sot-Weed Factor he
    passed from most promising to the best, most achieved
    author of the new generation; however, his "disciplined in-
    telligence . . ., wild invention and outrageous wit" iso-
    late him from his contemporaries. Fiedler wonders where
    is the center against which Barth defines himself.

1965

1   ANON. Review of The Sot-Weed Factor. National Observer
    (10 October), p. 22.

Magnificent with impossibly complicated plot. Calls the work a "mammoth piece of escapism."

2   ANON. "The Black Humorists." Time, 85 (12 February), 94-96.
    Barth discussed with other authors. Mentions The Sot-Weed Factor. Barth is intellectual and ironic, but not interested in social satire. Work is baudy and inventive.

3   ENCK, JOHN. "John Barth: An Interview, 17 April 1965." Wisconsin Studies in Contemporary Literature, 6 (Winter/Spring), 3-14.
    Barth discusses the nihilistic comic novel, his writing techniques, structure and form. Talks about classic and contemporary authors he admires and those he doesn't. Barth expounds on his philosophical ideas of reality. Sees The Floating Opera, End of the Road and The Sot-Weed Factor as a series of nihilistic novels. Giles Goat-Boy is to be a "new old testament, a comic old testament."

4   HICKS, G. Review of The Floating Opera, End of the Road and The Sot-Weed Factor. Saturday Review, 48 (3 July), 23.
    Sees The Floating Opera and End of the Road as questioning human values and motives. Barth shows lively intelligence and fresh imagination. Hicks is impressed with Barth's playfully used erudition in The Sot-Weed Factor. This work is his most resourceful attempt to present the human predicament.

5   HYMAN, STANLEY EDGAR. "John Barth's First Novel." New Leader (12 April), pp. 20-31.
    Talks about The Sot-Weed Factor and The Floating Opera. Praises both works; much of The Sot-Weed Factor was present in bud form in The Floating Opera. Hyman cannot conceive of a limit to Barth's eventual achievement.

6   KOSTELANETZ, RICHARD. "The Point is That Life Doesn't Have Any Point." New York Times Book Review, 6 June, pp. 3, 28, 30.
    Discussion of absurd literature. Barth's The Sot-Weed Factor mentioned. In common with other authors discussed, Barth finds more disorder than continuity. Doubts standard versions of the past and undercuts literary pretentions. Life as a whole is absurd. Novels achieve metaphysical pertinence.

7   _____. "Notes on the American Short Story Today." The Minnesota Review, 5:214-221.

1965

Barth only briefly mentioned as an absurd author who, in novel form, takes on history itself.

8 MILLER, RUSSELL H. "The Sot-Weed Factor: A Contemporary Mock-Epic." Critique, 8 (Winter), 88-100.

Miller points out that no critics have analyzed The Sot-Weed Factor from a structural point of view. Miller illustrates the mock-epic devices which Barth uses. Included are 16 parallels between The Sot-Weed Factor and Homer's Odyssey to show how Barth uses situations of ancient epic for comic effect.

9 RUBIN, LOUIS D., JR. "Notes on the Literary Scene: Their Own Language." Harpers, 230 (April), 173-175.

Examines Southern writers today and their break with tradition. Barth represents great break. The Floating Opera, End of the Road, and The Sot-Weed Factor show Barth's idea that the line between "comedy and tragedy, heroic and absurd, is blurred in its every manifestation." His comedy is rare for a Post-WW II Southern writer.

10 STUBBS, JOHN C. "John Barth as a Novelist of Ideas: The Themes of Value and Identity." Critique, 8 (Winter), 101-116.

The Floating Opera, End of the Road, The Sot-Weed Factor show manipulations of material to set forth ideas. Raises questions of value and identity. The Floating Opera analyzed in terms of "nihilistic comedy" and The End of the Road in terms of "nihilistic tragedy"--both terms of Barth. The Sot-Weed Factor seen as Barth's most satisfactory and complete treatment of value and identity. Approach is negative. Short story "Ambrose His Mark" is a reiteration of human condition. Barth views man as living in an irrational universe where absolute values cannot exist.

1966

1 ALTER, ROBERT. "The Apocalyptic Temper." Commentary, 41 (June), 61-66.

Barth's The Sot-Weed Factor mentioned as one novel (among others) which illustrates the "picaresque version of the apocalypse." Alter suggests that recent American literature has told less than the truth because of its apocalyptic postures. Seen as a form, not interested in facts of history or human nature. Examines apocalyptic concept in terms of its being a Jewish invention.

Writings about John Barth, 1956-1973

2   ANON. Review of <u>Giles Goat-Boy</u>. <u>Booklist</u>, 63 (15 November),
     363.
          Summary of plot. Calls novel "original in concept, com-
     plex in structure and plot." Book will be limited to so-
     phisticated readers who appreciate inventiveness and are
     not deterred by naturalism.

3   ANON. Review of <u>Giles Goat-Boy</u>. <u>Choice</u>, 3 (October), 632.
          Mentions <u>The Sot-Weed Factor</u>. Compares Barth to Swift
     and Nabokov for cool savagery and use of language. Recom-
     mended for all collections of serious fiction.

4   ANON. Review of <u>Giles Goat-Boy</u>. <u>Kirkus</u>, 24 (June), 550.
          Sees novel as an elaborate conceit with the final major
     one being Barth's assumption that readers will tolerate any-
     thing for any length of time merely because it is "awfully
     philosophical and terribly clever."

5   ANON. Review of <u>Giles Goat-Boy</u>. <u>Teachers College Record</u>, 68
     (November), 185.
          Recommends the novel for its teaching value. "Vast,
     comic, puzzling with echoes of whole worlds' history and
     literature summoned up."

6   ANON. "Around the Arts." <u>National Observer</u>, 5 (29 August),
     17.
          Brief review of <u>Giles Goat-Boy</u>. Giant allegorical novel
     whose "prose ripples like poetry." Most talked about book
     of the summer.

7   ANON. "Black Bible." <u>Time</u>, 88 (5 August), 92.
          Review of <u>Giles Goat-Boy</u>. Parable similar to Dante.
     "Pilgrimage within an invented cosmology." Bible which
     proceeds to confusion not revelation. As in earlier novels
     he says all that is true is that which the believer's na-
     ture says is true.

8   ANON. "Heroic Comedy." <u>Newsweek</u>, 68 (8 August), 81.
          Review of <u>Giles Goat-Boy</u>. Mentions <u>The Floating Opera</u>,
     <u>End of the Road</u> and <u>The Sot-Weed Factor</u>. Novel confirms
     Barth's reputation as most "prodigally gifted comic novel-
     ist . . . in English today." Brief interview with Barth
     who states that he begins with the premise of "the end of
     literature" and turns it against itself. Goes back to ar-
     tificial frame and long connected tales. Interested in
     myth of hero.

1966

9   ANON. "Year of the Fact." Newsweek, 68 (19 December), 117A.
Review of Giles Goat-Boy. "Mad comic epic." Giles
searches through world for his destiny, deterred not even
by the devil. Barth is a novelist with outrageous and
prodigal gifts.

10   BALLIETT, W. "Rub-a-Dub-Dub." New Yorker, 42 (10 December),
234.
Review of Giles Goat-Boy. Characters have no breath and
spirit, symbolism transparent, prose is arched and labored.
"Ring of self-justification deafening."

11   BANNON, B. A. Review of The Sot-Weed Factor. Publisher's
Weekly, 190 (14 November), 111.
Mentions Giles Goat-Boy. Reissue of the novel timed to
tie in with Barth's increasing critical stature since publication of Giles. He has acquired a considerable audience.

12   BEAGLE, P. S. "John Barth: Long Reach, Near Miss." Holiday,
40 (September), 131-132.
Mentions The Floating Opera, End of the Road, The Sot-
Weed Factor, and Giles Goat-Boy. The similarity of novels
more striking than their differences. Characters forever
hounded by proposition that value is impossible in an irrational world. Giles is a fascinating failure. Flawed
characterizations never transcend their state as symbols.

13   BYRD, SCOTT. "Giles Goat-Boy Visited." Critique, 9:108-112.
Critical article on Giles Goat-Boy. Mentions The Sot-
Weed Factor. Barth deliberately creates an extended work
of prose fiction which continues confessional, romance,
anatomy, and in Frye's terminology, a sacred book. Byrd
uses quotes and excerpts to show how Giles fits this latter
category. The confessional mode places the book's focus on
the hero and shifts the reader's attitude from mockery to
acceptance. Mythic parallels clash with modern ideology to
show that heroism may be futile or comic, but it remains
noble. In spite of the blending of forms, density of
method, and scope of materials, Byrd feels that there is
an ultimate unity in Giles which lifts it above artistic
ambition to aesthetic success.

14   CORBETT, E. P. Review of Giles Goat-Boy. America, 115
(17 September), 290.
Mentions The Sot-Weed Factor. Parallels myths in classical, medieval and Biblical literature. Allegory fun for
Ph.D. candidates. Reviewers stunned and bored, but at
times overall imagery admirable.

15 DAVIS, D. M. "Mr. Barth is a Grand Tease in the Rippling and
   Rolling Giles." National Observer, 5 (1 August), 19.
       Mentions The Sot-Weed Factor, End of the Road, and The
   Floating Opera. Barth put strains found in previous novels
   together in Giles. Prose exquisite. Only study can tell
   whether novel has a central purpose or whether it is one
   of those great ideas out of control.

16 DONOGHUE, DENIS. "Grand Old Opry." New York Review of Books
   (18 August), pp. 25-26.
       Review of Giles Goat-Boy. Mentions The Floating Opera,
   End of the Road, The Sot-Weed Factor. All Barth's novels
   read like operas. Giles begins promisingly enough but
   drifts into boredom. The Floating Opera is an interesting
   first book, Sot-Weed Factor a remarkable achievement, End
   of the Road not good, and Giles too long and tedious.

17 FEATHERSTONE, J. "John Barth as Jonathan Swift." New
   Republic, 155 (3 September), 17.
       Review of Giles Goat-Boy. Mentions The Floating Opera,
   The Sot-Weed Factor, and End of the Road. Novel is a 710-
   page "epic snooze." Barth's talents not disputed, but his
   mode doesn't work in Giles.

18 FREMONT-SMITH, ELIOT. "The Surfacing of Mr. Barth (Laughter)."
   New York Times, 3 August, p. 35.
       Review of Giles Goat-Boy. Mentions The Floating Opera,
   The End of the Road, The Sot-Weed Factor. Defines genius
   as one "who, by force of will and wild connections in the
   mind, intoxicates." Barth qualifies. As to controversy
   engendered by book, it doesn't matter. With Barth "par-
   take, eat, quaff, enjoy."

19 GARIS, ROBERT. "What Happened to John Barth?" Commentary,
   4 (October), 89-95.
       Garis admires End of the Road and The Floating Opera.
   Felt betrayed when The Sot-Weed Factor and Giles Goat-Boy
   turned out to be bad. Deliberately tedious, boring, and
   Barth's methods fail to achieve philosophical intentions.
   First two novels show impressive gift for embodying ideas
   in ordinary material of fiction. Barth's change of method
   for Garis amounts to Barth's deciding to stop being an
   artist. Has lost any capacity for self-criticism.

20 HARDING, W. Review of Giles Goat-Boy. Library Journal, 91
   (August), 3762.
       Mentions The Floating Opera, End of the Road, and The
   Sot-Weed Factor. Would have been a good novella, but falls
   of its own weight. Hope for better next time.

1966

21 HICKS, G. Review of Giles Goat-Boy. Saturday Review, 49
(6 August), 21.
Mentions The Floating Opera, The Sot-Weed Factor, and
End of the Road. Hicks sees Barth as one modern author who
has a great intellect and uses it. Giles is a philosophical novel investigating the nature of man and the nature of
the cosmos. As an allegory the novel is compared to Melville's Mardi. Giles has greatness; whether great success
or great failure, Hicks isn't sure. Like Giles, he finds
it difficult to distinguish between the two.

22 HILL, WILLIAM B., S.J. Review of Giles Goat-Boy. America,
115 (26 November), 706.
"Intelligent, witty parable . . . reverent and blas-
phemous, scatological. . . ." Novel's message seems to be
"live and be human." Because it is esoteric, its popular-
ity is a mystery.

23 HYMAN, STANLEY EDGAR. "The American Adam." In Standards: A
Chronicle of Books for Our Time. New York: Horizon Press,
pp. 204-208.
Critical review of The Sot-Weed Factor. Book is slow
starting and too long but, for the most part, wonderfully
funny. Hyman lists, along with page numbers, the episodes
which he considers especially funny. Hyman sees as Barth's
literary sources Candide, Rabelais, Don Quixote, etc. Also
Tarzan, Rover Boys and Keystone Comedies. Barth's talent
and learning are formidable.

24 KIELY, BENEDICT. "Ripeness was Not All: John Barth's Giles
Goat-Boy." Hollins Critic, 8 (December), 1-12.
Analysis of characters in End of the Road, The Sot-Weed
Factor, and Giles Goat-Boy. Praises Barth's lyricism. Now
that we've had a Barthian picaresque and a Barthian Gothic,
will we have a Barthian cosy Victorian?

25 KITCHING, J. "Forecasts." Publisher's Weekly, 189 (23 May),
81.
Review of Giles Goat-Boy. Long satiric novel both bawdy
and symbolic. Appeal is coolly intellectual, but plot is
fantastic.

26 KLEIN, M. "Gods and Goats." Reporter, 35 (22 September), 60.
Review of Giles Goat-Boy. Mentions The Sot-Weed Factor,
The Floating Opera, and End of the Road. Novel is monu-
mental and imposing. Comedy is impersonal. Analyzed alle-
gorically. Giles is a reconciliation of existential problems set forth in previous works.

27   McCOHN, PEARLMARIE. "The Revised New Syllabus and the
          Unrevised Old." Denver Quarterly (Autumn), pp. 136-141.
              Review of Giles Goat-Boy. Brilliant and clever, but
          most self-conscious. Satirical parallels funny but super-
          ficial. Joke finally on the reader—demands unwilling sus-
          pension of disbelief and willing suspension of realistic
          values.

28   MALIN, IRVING. "Son of a Computer." Progressive (November),
          p. 46.
              Review of Giles Goat-Boy. Barth inverts conventional
          forms to show how they hide terrifying reality. Giles'
          comic strategies shape complex philosophical and metaphysi-
          cal issues. Barth is inventive, fantastic, farcical, and
          serious.

29   _____. Review of Giles Goat-Boy. Commonweal, 85
          (2 December), 270.
              Mentions The Sot-Weed Factor. Barth is apocalyptic.
          Takes on the universe itself. Combats the computer, symbol
          of present doom. Asks the questions, who is responsible?
          and can we laugh?

30   MERAS, PHYLLIS. "John Barth: A Truffle No Longer." New York
          Times Book Review (7 August), p. 22.
              Interview with Barth. Discussions of The Sot-Weed Fac-
          tor and Giles Goat-Boy. Barth talks about university life.
          Some biographical material.

31   MORSE, J. M. "Fiction Chronicle." Hudson Review, 19
          (August), 507.
              Review of Giles Goat-Boy. Novel is undergraduate humor—
          magazine fiction. Barth's values are those of "a tame
          goat."

32   NOLAND, RICHARD W. "John Barth and the Novel of Comic
          Nihilism." Wisconsin Studies in Contemporary Literature,
          7 (Autumn), 239-257.
              Noland examines Barth's The Floating Opera, End of the
          Road, and The Sot-Weed Factor in relation to his thesis
          that the novels are in the nihilistic and existential tra-
          dition. Barth is one novelist who takes the fact of ni-
          hilism as subject matter without developing a value system.
          His novels show the existential ideas of relativity of
          values, suicide as a philosophical problem, and the mixture
          of tragedy and comedy which characterizes absurdity. Noland
          feels Barth's mode of parody reaches fullest development in
          The Sot-Weed Factor. In addition to his previous themes of

1966

existence and identity, Barth adds innocence in this novel.
Noland sees as flaws in Barth's work the sentimentality and
forced happy ending in The Floating Opera, a weakness in
characterization in End of the Road and the perverseness of
parody and continued thinness of character in The Sot-Weed
Factor.

33 O'CONNELL, S. "Goat Gambit at the University." Nation, 203
    (5 September), 193.
        Review of Giles Goat-Boy. Mentions The Floating Opera,
    End of the Road, and The Sot-Weed Factor. Logic yielding
    to paradox extended in Barth's fourth novel. Intention to
    create "not so brave new world" in grandly imagined con-
    struct. Style ignores own thematic conclusion. Ideas be-
    come tedious.

34 POIRIER, RICHARD. Review of Giles Goat-Boy. Choice, 3
    (October), 632.
        Mentions The Sot-Weed Factor. Barth's "cool savagery
    and incomparable use of language." Compared to Nabokov and
    Swift.

35 RUBIN, LOUIS D., JR. "The Curious Death of the Novel: or,
    What to Do About Tired Literary Critics." Kenyon Review,
    28 (June), 305-325.
        Barth mentioned briefly as one of a group of highly
    talented writers exploring "already discovered ground to
    see whether anything important has been overlooked." Barth
    just beginning to be appreciated.

36 SAMUELS, CHARLES THOMAS. "John Barth: A Buoyant Denial of
    Relevance." Commonweal, 85 (21 October), 80-82.
        Review of Giles Goat-Boy. Mentions The Floating Opera,
    End of the Road, and The Sot-Weed Factor. First two novels
    poor in "novelistic pleasure." Characters are sticks.
    Plot inorganic, ideas banal. Sot-Weed Factor solipsistic,
    labored virtuosity, prurient vigor, and has vulgar ease of
    invitation. Giles is 710 pages of allegory written in
    prose reminiscent of that written by computer.

37 SCHLUETER, P. "Puncturing the Gods." Christian Century, 83
    (21 September), 1149.
        Review of Giles Goat-Boy. Mentions The Sot-Weed Factor.
    Academic and religious metaphors briefly examined. Barth
    succeeds well in puncturing false gods.

38 SCHOLES, ROBERT. "George is My Name." New York Times Book
    Review (7 August), pp. 1, 22.

22

Review of Giles Goat-Boy. Mentions The Sot-Weed Factor.
Both novels stamp Barth as the best present writer of fiction and one of the best ever. Giles great in originality
of structure and language. Barth makes few concessions to
the dull or uneducated. His audience has to be the same
as those prepared by Joyce, Proust, Mann, and Faulkner.

39   _____. "Disciple of Scheherazade." New York Times Book
Review, 71 (8 May), 5, 22.
Mentions The Floating Opera, End of the Road, and The
Sot-Weed Factor. Barth a "bawdy allegorist" whose works
prove that the novel is not dead but "phoenixed." Only
criticism is that Barth sacrifices emotional depth as he
moves us fast and far, but not deep.

40   SCHOTT, W. "A Black Comedy to Offend Everyone." Life, 61
(12 August), 10.
Review of Giles Goat-Boy. Mentions The Sot-Weed Factor.
"Long, boring, frustrating . . . , only mitigating quality
is Barth's wild originality." Loses because his satire
does not identify values.

41   SHAPIRO, J. L. Review of Giles Goat-Boy. Best Sellers, 26
(1 October), 231.
Novel confirms promise of The Sot-Weed Factor, but will
be appreciated only by a select few. Plot difficult to pin
down. Themes as varied as life--parts will hold any reader,
but whole can be taken only as a "project."

42   STUART, DABNEY. "A Service to the University." Shenandoah,
18 (Autumn), 96-99.
Compares similarities of Giles Goat-Boy and The Sot-Weed
Factor. Both concerned with masks, deceptions, and illu-
sions. Structurally both novels share elements of picaresque. Allegory introduced in Giles. Stuart rates Giles
with Moby Dick as best fiction yet written by an American.

1967

1   ANON. Review of The Floating Opera (rev. ed.). Publisher's
Weekly, 191 (6 March), 73.
Mentions The Sot-Weed Factor and Giles Goat-Boy. Barth's
foreword seen as petulant. However, it remains an interesting first novel by an author of promise.

2   ANON. Review of Giles Goat-Boy. Publisher's Weekly, 191
(26 June), 68.

1967

>Mentions The Floating Opera and The Sot-Weed Factor.
Discusses the diverse critical reviews of the novel and
mentions that Giles sold 50,000 in hard cover and was dis-
tributed by two major book clubs.

3 ANON. Review of Giles Goat-Boy. Saturday Review, 50
   (30 September), 47.
   >Brief review. "Weighty, mystic, allegoric."

4 ANON. Review of Giles Goat-Boy. Virginia Quarterly Review,
   43 (Winter), viii.
   >Barth revolutionizes the novel form in "structure, style
   and content." Makes no concessions to the general reader
   who can not match the author in pedantry. Persistent
   reader will be rewarded.

5 ANON. Review of The Sot-Weed Factor (rev. ed.). Choice, 4
   (June), 418.
   >Recommends the 1960 edition. "Modern satirical classic."

6 ANON. "Existentialist Comedian." Time (17 March), p. 109.
   >Mentions The Floating Opera, End of the Road, The Sot-
   Weed Factor, and Giles Goat-Boy. Article is about Barth.
   His books trace the process of an anti-novelist. Comments
   by Barth on literature.

7 ANON. "John Barth: Goat-Boy's Father." Playboy, 14 (March),
   142.
   >Mentions The Sot-Weed Factor. Giles is an "improbable
   comedy." Short biography of Barth included.

8 ANON. "The Joker is Wild." Times Literary Supplement
   (30 March), p. 261.
   >Review of Giles Goat-Boy. Barth thrives on "vast reper-
   toire of juvenile blasphemy, sophomoric sex jokes, rhyming
   slang."

9 BURGESS, A. "Caprine Messiah." Spectator, 218 (31 March),
   369.
   >Review of Giles Goat-Boy. Mentions The Sot-Weed Factor.
   Latter novel represented one direction the novel might take
   to stay alive. Mocked its subject matter and itself. Giles
   implies that form must revert to its mixed origins and mock
   even those. It makes much contemporary British fiction
   look light weight.

10 CORKE, H. "New Novels." Listener, 77 (30 March), 437.
   >Contrary to most authors whose gigantic novels score low
   on content and high in length, Barth's Giles Goat-Boy scores

high in both. Sees theme as "grotesque parody of Christian
scripture and man's re-education by the animal." Modifies
reader's received view of things forever.

11   HANEY, P. Review of reissue of The Floating Opera. Denver
      Quarterly, 2 (Summer), 170-171.
          Theme is still fresh; new ending is tougher and more
      honest. Weaving of outlandish web around dry philosophical
      idea.

12   JOHNSON, B. S. "Giles Fitz WESCAC Fitz Englit." Books and
      Bookmen, 12 (April), 60.
          Review of Giles Goat-Boy. Mentions The Sot-Weed Factor.
      In both novels Barth applies academic techniques to con-
      temporary politics, religion, and philosophy. While nar-
      rative gifts are brilliant, the main intention is obscure.
      Criticism is that Giles is "a book made out of other books;
      . . . it recapitulates without innovating."

13   KOSTELANETZ, RICHARD. "New American Fiction Reconsidered."
      Tri-Quarterly, 8:279-286.
          Talks about novels read past and present. Barth's Giles
      Goat-Boy not as good as The Sot-Weed Factor, but still first
      rate. Most of its deficiencies come from inability to match
      realization with intention.

14   LEVINE, PAUL. "The Intemperate Zone: The Climate of
      Contemporary American Fiction." Massachusetts Review, 8
      (Summer), 505-523.
          Mentions The Sot-Weed Factor and Giles Goat-Boy. Sees
      line between fantasy and reality fading. Modern America
      is incredible in its reality; reporter has become satirist
      due to his material. Barth seeks new resolution of reality
      problem by "ironic fusion of historical fact and black fan-
      tasy." Pushes frontiers in an effort to find form appropri-
      ate to contemporary experience.

15   LIFSON, H. "Giles Goat Bore." North American Review, 4
      (November), inside cover.
          Giles worth mentioning only for its inexplicable criti-
      cal praise and the necessity of rebutting the precept that
      quixotic gestures against science may save us. Theme is
      trite and worthy of an undergraduate frat skit.

16   LODGE, DAVID. "Goatscape with Figures." Tablet (8 April),
      p. 383.
          Sees novel from two perspectives: 1) as an example of
      "novelistic synthesis" held together by realism; 2) as the

1967

ultimate "campus novel." Barth fascinated by paradoxes,
the ultimate one being sexual. Book an "exciting and . . .
an encouraging achievement."

17 McGUINNESS, FRANK. Review of Giles Goat-Boy. London Magazine
    (May), p. 89.
        Mentions The Sot-Weed Factor. Giles is a massive tome
    in which the industry of the writer is matched only by the
    persistence of the reader. Fails as satire because it is
    burdened by idiotic detail.

18 MacNAMARA, D. "Scape Goat." New Statesman, 73 (31 March),
    442.
        Review of Giles Goat-Boy. Wordy excess that fatigues.
    Mentions The Sot-Weed Factor. Summarizes plot.

19 PETERSEN, C. "Ecstatic Agonies." Books Today, 4 (20 August),
    13.
        Reviews the reviews of Giles Goat-Boy. Shows the diver-
    sity of the reviews.

20 SCHOLES, ROBERT. "Fabulation and Epic Vision." In The
    Fabulators. New York: Oxford University Press,
    pp. 134-173.
        Scholes calls Giles Goat-Boy a work of genuine epic vi-
    sion, designed to startle us into new perceptions of the
    epic hero and savior. Scholes uses passages to show how
    Barth's vision is related to his use of language. As the
    two are thematically related, something of the book's
    structure is also revealed. Rest of article concerns the
    basic allegorical metaphors and their appropriateness. Ex-
    amines the allegorical levels of meaning, using historical,
    sociological, psychological, philosophical, and theological
    dimensions. Tension between philosophical and mythic views
    of existence seen as heart of Barth's work.

21 SHUTTLEWORTH, M. "New Novels." Punch, 252 (5 April), 504.
        Review of Giles Goat-Boy. Huge academic spoof. Clever
    at parody but novel creaks "like Lyly's Euphues."

22 SKERRETT, JOSEPH TAYLOR, JR. "Dostoievsky, Nathanael West,
    and Some Contemporary American Fiction." The University of
    Dayton Review, 4:23-36.
        Contrasts the "Black Humorists" and the authors of "the
    lost Generation." New novelists are broadly and irrever-
    ently comic. Also discursive and intellectual in a way the
    novel has not been for some time. Sees influence of eigh-
    teenth century English prose fiction. Sees precedent also

in pessimism of Twain and Nathanael West. West's four short novels connected to Black humorists by tone, "clarity, documentary detachment and deadpan satire." Mentions The Floating Opera and The Sot-Weed Factor in illustrating his points.

23 TANNER, TONY. "The Hoax That Joke Bilked." Partisan Review, 34 (Winter), 102-109.
    Mentions The Floating Opera, End of the Road, The Sot-Weed Factor, and Giles Goat-Boy. Novels contain potentially serious issues but get caught up in tone of farce and ridicule. Barth's free-wheeling inventiveness is dazzling, but Tanner feels that the "arbitrary unimpeded sport of sheer mind" does not enrich a novel. In Giles it is damaging.

24 WILSON, J. and ANTHONY BURGESS. "History and Myth." In The Novel Now: A Student's Guide to Contemporary Fiction. London: Faber and Faber, p. 136.
    The Sot-Weed Factor does something original in the historical field. Finds absurdity in history. Burgess admires Barth's courage in being a scholar who mocks scholarship.

1968

1 ADAMS, PHOEBE. Review of Lost in the Funhouse. Atlantic, 222 (October), 150.
   "Amusing experiments, Homeric excursions, and the revelation that Mr. Barth can write verse just like . . . Rudyard Kipling."

2 ANON. Review of Lost in the Funhouse. Kirkus, 36 (1 August), 836.
   Praises Sot-Weed Factor and Giles Goat-Boy, but Barth is not at his best in this "uneven and randomly connected collection of short stories." Only title story should stand the test of time.

3 ANON. Review of Lost in the Funhouse. Publisher's Weekly, 194 (29 July), 56.
   Mentions Giles Goat-Boy and The Sot-Weed Factor. Multimedia fiction. Barth experiments wildly and at times appears like a pretentious put-on. Results more curious than rewarding.

4 ANON. "Liebestodd." Times Literary Supplement (10 October), p. 1161.

1968

> Review of The Floating Opera. Mentions The Sot-Weed Factor, Giles Goat-Boy, and End of the Road. British edition. Cool work but remains a construct where not everything comes off. Premises deployed but not proven. Total effect is entertaining but heartless.

5   APPEL, A., JR. "The Art of Artifice." Nation, 207 (28 October), 441.

> Review of Lost in the Funhouse. Mentions The Floating Opera and Giles Goat-Boy. Barth one of the authors who produces cerebral, fantastic fiction with constantly evolving forms. Metaphysics are the rule. Barth's efforts include intermedia art.

6   ARDERY, P. P. "Books in Brief." National Review, 20 (3 December), 1230.

> Review of Lost in the Funhouse. Mentions The Floating Opera, End of the Road, and Giles Goat-Boy. Barth now an allegorist and imagist. New Barth is too much a creator of language and not of life.

7   AXTHELM, P. "Tiny Odyssey." Newsweek, 72 (30 September), 106.

> Review of Lost in the Funhouse. A finely drawn picture of the creative process. Theme is mythic. Dullness fleeting in Barth's rich prose.

8   BOYERS, ROBERT. "Attitudes Toward Sex in American 'High Culture.'" Annals of the American Academy of Political and Social Sciences (March), pp. 36-52.

> Boyers analyzes sexual themes and attitudes found in the fiction of the last decade. Barth is seen as treating sex as an evasion of reality. Barth's attitude toward sex reflects his world view. Irony, detachment and cynicism are shown in End of the Road, the novel Boyers picks as representative of Barth's attitudes.

9   BYRD, SCOTT. "A Separate War: Camp and Black Humor in Recent American Fiction." Language Quarterly, 70:7-10.

> Byrd's thesis is that camp and Black Humor cannot be reconciled with the term satire. Camp is defined as "a genuine delight in the discovery of a passionately misconceived object." Black Humor involves "satiric expression of an absolute moral judgment . . . through fictional gestures of almost total hostility." Barth's hero in Giles Goat-Boy is mentioned as an example of a Black Humor hero's withdrawal from struggle to redeem world.

10   DAVENPORT, G. "Like Nothing Nameable." New York Times Book
        Review, 73 (20 October), 4.
           Review of Lost in the Funhouse. Mentions Giles Goat-Boy
        and The Sot-Weed Factor. Barth's prose designs are like
        nothing we can name; but experimentation does not change
        style which is still plastic and delightful.

11   DAVIS, DOUGLAS M. "The End is a Beginning for Barth's
        Funhouse." National Observer (16 September), p. 19.
           Interview with Barth. Talks about Lost in the Funhouse.
        Mentions Giles Goat-Boy, The Floating Opera, The Sot-Weed
        Factor, End of the Road. Discusses cyclical quality of
        novel, McLuhan, and faction for "tape" and "live voice."
        Short biography included.

12   DISER, PHILIP F. "The Historical Ebenezer Cooke." Critique,
        10:48-59.
           Diser attempts to show that Barth is historically ac-
        curate as far as known facts about Ebenezer Cooke's life,
        and that he uses Cooke's original poem as a catalyst to his
        own imagination in writing The Sot-Weed Factor.

13   ELLIOTT, GEORGE P. "Destroyers, Defilers, and Confusers of
        Men." Atlantic Monthly, 6 (December), 74-80.
           Elliott distinguishes three types of nihilistic writers:
        the destroyers, defilers, and confusers. Barth was destruc-
        tive in End of the Road, defiling in The Sot-Weed Factor,
        and moved to confusion in Giles Goat-Boy. Third rate con-
        fuser. The ideology makes the novel vague and more boring
        than confusing.

14   FIEDLER, LESLIE A. "The Anti-Pocahontas of Us All." In The
        Return of the Vanishing American. New York: Stein and
        Day, pp. 150-153.
           Fiedler sees the new Western beginning with John Barth's
        The Sot-Weed Factor in 1960. The prim Protestant version
        of Pocahontas gives way to a stripped, dusky-skinned
        temptress. Barth compared to Voltaire and Anatole France--
        "a defiler and riddler and cutter." Barth creates an anti-
        stereotype of our beginnings in Virginia. The sexual en-
        counter is more an assault than an act of love, hence a
        truer metaphor of our relations with the Indians. At the
        end, Pocahontas waits for her lover. The anti-Pocahontas
        has appeared in the new Western since as a whore begging to
        be screwed. Fiedler gives other examples.

15   FREMONT-SMITH, E. "Make it New." New York Times, 16 October,
        p. 49.

1968

>Review of <u>Lost in the Funhouse</u>. Novel almost wholly
concerned with technical relationships. Playful, mathematical puzzler. Tones up imaginative literary art.

16 GRAFF, GERALD E. "Mythotherapy and Modern Poetics."
<u>Tri-Quarterly</u>, 11:76-90.
>Uses Barth's <u>End of the Road</u> as a starting point for
contemporary poetic theory. Graff concludes that until we
recognize that reason is the only method of dealing with
unreason we cannot transcend exclusions and antitheses of
current theory.

17 GRAHAM, K. Review of <u>The Floating Opera</u>. <u>Listener</u>, 80
(3 October), 449.
>First British publication seen as small beside the giant
<u>Sot-Weed Factor</u>, but shows same "Shandean vigour and dis-
array." Expertise and aplomb startling for a first novel.
Center of novels remains an intellectual attitude and
leaves reader "detached, mildly intrigued, and turning
aside to something else."

18 GROSS, BEVERLY. "The Anti-Novels of John Barth." <u>Chicago
Review</u>, 20 (November), 95-109.
>Rereading of Barth produces exasperation not enlighten-
ment. His fiction moves toward repudiation of narrative
art. <u>The Floating Opera</u>, <u>End of the Road</u>, <u>The Sot-Weed
Factor</u>, and <u>Giles Goat-Boy</u> become progressively nihilistic
but paradoxically humorous. All novels have roles as central motif. Gross supports this thesis by detailed analysis of <u>The Sot-Weed Factor</u> and <u>Giles Goat-Boy</u>.

19 HARDING, WALTER. Review of <u>Lost in the Funhouse</u>. <u>Library
Journal</u>, 93 (15 September), 3153.
>Mentions <u>Giles Goat-Boy</u> and <u>The Sot-Weed Factor</u>. Also
<u>The Floating Opera</u>. "Group of pseudo-Homeric tales . . .
bloated and over written. . . ."

20 HICKS, G. Review of <u>Lost in the Funhouse</u>. <u>Saturday Review</u>,
51 (28 September), 31.
>Mentions <u>Giles Goat-Boy</u>. Hicks believes that many
writers sacrifice their talent in a rush to be original.
Barth is not one of these. He has proven an equal to the
traditionalists and has won the right to be different.
Though some of the experiments in <u>Funhouse</u> don't get any-
where, Barth's first-rate imagination comes through. Two
years after review of <u>Giles</u>, Hicks is now sure it is one
of the most important novels of our time.

Writings about John Barth, 1956-1973

21   _____. "Fables for People Who Can Hear With Their Eyes."
         Time, 92 (27 September), 100.
              Review of Lost in the Funhouse. Mentions The Sot-Weed
         Factor and Giles Goat-Boy. Designed for multi-media per-
         formance. Work of "highly significant irrelevance."

22   HILL, HAMLIN. "Black Humor: Its Cause and Cure." The
         Colorado Quarterly, 17 (Summer), 57-64.
              Barth mentioned as one of a group of contemporary authors
         who are classified indiscriminantly as Black Humorists.
         None of his works is mentioned. Hill's article attempts to
         define Black Humor and examines works which illustrate his
         definition.

23   HILL, W. B. Review of Lost in the Funhouse. America
         (30 November), p. 563.
              Not Barth at his best but stories can be read "simply,
         silently, happily." Allusive and compelling.

24   HOLDER, ALAN. "'What Marvelous Plot . . . Was Afoot?'
         History in Barth's The Sot-Weed Factor." American
         Quarterly, 20 (Fall), 596-604.
              Holder shows how Barth takes liberties with historical
         records as appear in Archives of Maryland. Book's ideas,
         even when seriously offered, are inadequately felt. Novel
         basically a performance with history existing primarily as
         "repository of details and plots that Barth wants to master
         and outdo."

25   LEE, L. L. "Some Uses of Finnegans Wake in John Barth's The
         Sot-Weed Factor." James Joyce Quarterly, 5 (Winter),
         177-178.
              Compares quotes from both novels to present thesis that
         Finnegans Wake is one or both parents of The Sot-Weed Fac-
         tor. Joyce's sentences are essential to Barth's novel--re-
         inforcing themes and attitudes.

26   MURRAY, J. J. Review of Lost in the Funhouse. Best Sellers,
         28 (15 October), 282.
              Range and variety of stories overwhelming. Barth is a
         genius when using style for style's sake. Critics have
         charged that his writing lacks emotion. Murray says they
         miss an obvious point. Barth is most passionate about his
         writing.

27   POIRIER, RICHARD. "The Politics of Self-Parody." Partisan
         Review, 35 (Summer), 339-353.

1968

Literature of self-parody makes fun of itself as it goes
along. Makes fun of efforts to verify literary standards.
The only responsibility of literature is to be interesting
about its own inventions. Barth mentioned as one author
whose novels contend with our admiration for their thinking
about literature. The Sot-Weed Factor, Giles Goat-Boy, and
The Floating Opera are mentioned. Disappointing to put so
much effort into a book only to discover the author trying
as hard to turn you off as to turn you on.

28 PRICE, R. J. "New Novels." Punch, 255 (2 October), 487.
    Review of The Floating Opera. Mentions The Sot-Weed
    Factor. Marks former novel's British publication. "Rather
    self-indulgently wayward."

29 RABEN, JONATHON. The Technique of Modern Fiction. London:
    Edward Arnold Ltd., pp. 70-79, 138-144.
    Raban uses excerpts from the works of modern novelists
    to illustrate technique. Barth's End of the Road and The
    Sot-Weed Factor are included. The dialogue in the passage
    from End of the Road shows how Barth's writing strength in-
    volves us in an interview in which logic and cause win, but
    where we are simultaneously confronted with a world of ran-
    dom sensations and irrelevant speculation. The Sot-Weed
    Factor as a linguistic caricature conjures up a world so
    remote that it casts an ironic light on thinly disguised
    contemporary issues. Barth manages to join the eighteenth
    century bourgeois and the twentieth century existentialists
    by using language on one hand and topic on the other.

30 RICHARDSON, JACK. "Amusement and Revelation." New Republic
    (23 November), p. 30.
    Barth's methods in Lost in the Funhouse show his crafts-
    man's knowledge of narrative. Novel is good literature,
    gathering of notes about how literature is made and read,
    and an entertaining game of multiple reflections.

31 SCHOTT, W. "One Baffled Barth in Search of a Book." Life,
    65 (18 October), 8.
    Review of Lost in the Funhouse. Unfunny "autistic paro-
    dies of Greek classics." Mentions The Sot-Weed Factor and
    Giles Goat-Boy; after these Barth has nothing left to write
    about.

32 SCHULZ, MAX F. "Pop, Op, and Black Humor: The Aesthetics of
    Anxiety." College English, 30 (December), 230-241.
    Barth briefly mentioned as one author currently seeking
    to control the temporality inherent in literary form. The

32

Sot-Weed Factor and Giles Goat-Boy fix time in "endless
circularity."

33 SHAPIRO, STEPHEN A. "The Ambivalent Animal: Man in the
     Contemporary British and American Novel." The Centennial
     Review, 12:1-22.
          Shapiro cites psychological, sociological, political,
     and philosophical forces which have led to contemporary
     man's choice of "becoming a connoisseur of ambiguity or be-
     coming paralyzed." Barth's End of the Road is illustrative
     of novels which explore "the Janusian ambivalence of the
     universe." Sot-Weed Factor mentioned.

34 SMITH, HARRY. "Bestsellers Nobody Reads." Smith, 10
     (November), 182-185.
          Survey on books bought but not read. Barth's novels
     bought for prestige and display. Giles Goat-Boy--of 81
     purchased copies, only 7 read completely, 21 partially, and
     53 not read at all.

                              1969

1 ANON. Review of Lost in the Funhouse. Choice, 6 (April),
    210.
          Mentions Giles Goat-Boy. Barth's brilliance vitiated by
    excessive variations on a theme. Admirers may find it
    intriguing.

2 ANON. "John Barth Papers." The Quarterly Journal of the
    Library of Congress, 26:247-249.
          Relates content of John Barth's papers which includes
    literary manuscripts but no correspondence. Sixteen manu-
    script boxes consisting mainly of manuscripts of his four
    novels. At least two versions of each manuscript.

3 ANON. "Just for the Record." Times Literary Supplement
    (18 September), p. 1017.
          Review of Lost in the Funhouse. Synopsis of plot.
    "Barth's finest logical fantasies take wing from experience."

4 BAILEY, P. "Breaking the Rules." London Magazine (December),
    p. 109.
          Review of Lost in the Funhouse. Calls Giles "that vast
    slab of deadness." Lost in the Funhouse also manages to be
    overwritten and long-winded. Prose "arid rather than
    winged."

1969

5 BRADBURY, JOHN M. "Absurd Insurrection: The Barth-Percy
     Affair." South Atlantic Quarterly, 68 (Summer), 319-329.
        Bradbury contrasts Barth and Percy with Faulkner and
     Warren. The latter authors' characters' self-identity is
     unattainable without rebirth into a traditional value sys-
     tem. With Barth and Percy the old Agrarian-based values
     have disappeared. The new South is absurd, producing exis-
     tential despair, "cosmopsis, suicide."

6 DIPPIE, BRIAN W. "'His Visage Wild; His Form Exotick'; Indian
     Themes and Cultural Guilt in John Barth's The Sot-Weed
     Factor." American Quarterly, 21 (Spring), 113-121.
        Dippie uses excerpts from the novel to show that it is
     an exposé and exposition of some favorite American myths.
     In addition to this major theme of the search for identity
     in America, Barth incorporates the guilt felt for the In-
     dians as part of the American experience and investigates
     savagery versus civilization. Barth's purpose is satiric,
     but not destructive. He creates from fresh observation an
     appreciation of the complexities which constitute an
     American.

7 FENTON, J. "Barthist." New Statesman (19 September), p. 384.
        Review of Lost in the Funhouse. Mentions Giles Goat-Boy.
     Former's brevity not accompanied by simplicity. Strong
     thematic links between pieces seen as search for identity.
     "Most brilliant and inventive writer of our time."

8 FIEDLER, LESLIE A. "Cross the Border, Close the Gap."
     Playboy, 16 (December), 151, 230, 252-254, 256-258.
        The "gap" referred to in the title is the function of
     the modern novel as a closing of the gap between elite and
     mass culture or a movement away from genteel tradition to
     pop. Fiedler feels the Western, Science Fiction, and por-
     nography illustrate this. Barth's The Sot-Weed Factor and
     Giles Goat-Boy mentioned as Western and Science Fiction.
     Have to invent a new "new criticism" appropriate to post-
     Modernist fiction.

9 GARIS, R. "Fiction Chronicle." Hudson Review, 22 (Spring),
     148.
        Barth's genius shows when he writes End of the Road.
     The Sot-Weed Factor and Giles Goat-Boy are unreadable.
     Barth's language has come back to genuine and funny life
     in Lost in the Funhouse.

10 HARVEY, D. D. "Muddle-Brewed Fiction." Southern Review
     (Winter), p. 259.

Review of <u>Giles Goat-Boy</u>. Mentions <u>End of the Road</u> and <u>The Sot-Weed Factor</u>. The former novel's allegory tires one and is without force. "Life-denying."

11 HJORTSBERG, W. "John Barth in the Global Village." <u>Catholic World</u> (January), p. 188.
  Review of <u>Lost in the Funhouse</u>. Stories vary radically in technique yet achieve a unity. "Book a challenge and a delight."

12 HOOD, S. "Silver-Age Fun." <u>Listener</u> (18 September), p. 188.
  Review of <u>Lost in the Funhouse</u>. Reader should persevere to find "wit, humour and a fascinating play of mirrors as Barth steps behind the technique . . . to pose problems on the nature of existence and self-perception." Uses mythology to act out artist's inner drama. Easy to get lost, but there are extraordinary things to find in the funhouse.

13 LEMON, L. T. "Barth's Good Book." <u>Prairie Schooner</u> (Summer), p. 231.
  Review of <u>Lost in the Funhouse</u>. One theme through the pieces is the implication of being a creator. An "ungainly assortment" of modes and styles adds up to rich analysis of the problems of creator.

14 POIRIER, RICHARD. "A Literature of Law and Order." <u>Partisan Review</u>, 36:189-204.
  Problem of organizing self and destiny within contexts that impose self-developed literary traditions now shown in work of Mailer, Barth, and Pynchon, "tiresomely repetitious." <u>The End of the Road</u>, <u>Giles Goat-Boy</u>, and <u>Lost in the Funhouse</u> mentioned. In latest works Poirier sees Barth questioning authenticity of his work.

15 RYAN, MARJORIE. "Four Contemporary Satires and the Problem of Norms." <u>Satire Newsletter</u>, 6 (September), 40-46.
  Rebuttal to Peter Thorpe's statement that the satire of past 15 years is superficial and destructive, lacking norms. Barth's <u>The Floating Opera</u> cited as satire verging on irony. Commentary on life at any time but belongs to contemporary satire because positive values are emotional not intellectual.

16 SUTTON, HENRY. "Notes Toward the Destitution of Culture." <u>The Kenyon Review</u>, 30:108-115.
  Characterizes Barth's <u>Giles Goat-Boy</u> as a paranoid simplification of the world, giving suggestions about the way reality functions.

1969

17   TANNER, TONY. "No Exit." <u>Partisan Review</u>, 36:293-295,
         297-299.
              Review of <u>Lost in the Funhouse</u>. Novel, though brilliant,
         shows Barth has gone "astray in possibility." Barth cannot
         grasp any reality; all he touches turns to fiction. Men-
         tions Barth's uncertainty about relationship between worlds
         he invents and those he lives in. But Barth resists tempta-
         tion to abandon forms, definitions, and style.

18   TUBE, H. "Vivifiction." <u>Spectator</u> (20 September), p. 374.
              Review of <u>Lost in the Funhouse</u>. Admires precision of
         Barth's formal treatment but cannot warm to his voice.
         Heartiness cannot make up for lack of feeling.

19   WASSON, RICHARD. "Notes on a New Sensibility." <u>Partisan
         Review</u>, 36:460-477.
              Barth's <u>End of the Road</u> is "end of the road" for myth
         and metaphor as moderns understand it. Plot of ideological
         farce reveals the weakness of myth. Wasson states we have
         to develop a "mythoplastic and skeptical criticism aware of
         its artificiality."

20   WYLDER, DELBERT E. "Thomas Berger's <u>Little Big Man</u> as
         Literature." <u>Western American Literature</u>, 3 (Winter),
         273-284.
              Barthian recreation of a history of the absurd related
         to framework of <u>Little Big Man</u>. While Barthian in approach
         it is Western in attitude toward humanity and value.

1970

1   BRYANT, JERRY. <u>The Open Decision</u>. New York: The Free Press,
         pp. 286-299.
              Bryant uses contemporary novelists to show the values
         presupposed in their works do not express pessimism and
         disgust with the human condition. Rather, the conditions
         of man's existence, i.e., loneliness, alienation and pain,
         also serve to affirm his individuality and identity. John
         Barth's <u>End of the Road</u>, <u>Giles Goat-Boy</u>, <u>The Floating Opera</u>,
         and <u>The Sot-Weed Factor</u> are among the novels chosen to il-
         lustrate Bryant's point.

2   HAUCK, RICHARD B. "The Comic Christ and the Modern Reader."
         <u>College English</u>, 31 (February), 498-506.
              <u>Giles Goat-Boy</u> written by teacher and scholar reacting
         to other Christ figure books. Recurrence of Christ figure
         in a world where history doomed to be cyclical. Literature
         course in itself.

WRITINGS ABOUT JOHN BARTH, 1956-1973

3   HICKS, GRANVILLE. "John Barth." In Literary Horizons.
     New York: New York University Press, pp. 257-272.
       Three book reviews reprinted from Saturday Review. Af-
     terword by Hicks. He doubts if everyone who bought Giles
     Goat-Boy understood it. Barth is continuing to experiment.
     Hicks expects a good deal of fine work in the future.

4   JOSEPH, GERHARD. "John Barth." University of Minnesota
     Pamphlets on American Authors (91). Minneapolis:
     University of Minnesota Press. Also in Dictionary of
     American Literary Biography. New York: Scribner's, 1973.
       Critical analysis of The Floating Opera, The End of the
     Road, The Sot-Weed Factor, Giles Goat-Boy, and Lost in the
     Funhouse. Barth's themes do not undergo changes from work
     to work. Heroes try to find philosophical justification
     for life, look for values in a relativistic world and con-
     cern themselves with problems of freedom and reality. In-
     cluded is a selected bibliography.

5   KENNARD, JEAN E. "John Barth: Imitations of Imitations."
     Mosaic, 3 (Winter), 116-131.
       Examines existential ideas in Barth's works. The Float-
     ing Opera, The Sot-Weed Factor, and Giles Goat-Boy analyzed.
     Each of the heroes seeks to come to terms with existence.
     Technique brings about experience of absurd in reader.

6   MAJDIAK, DANIEL. "Barth and the Representation of Life."
     Criticism, 12 (Winter), 51-67.
       Majdiak states that Barth's later works have been ana-
     lyzed in terms of his "representation of life" but that no
     one has looked at his earlier novels from this perspective.
     Analyzes The Floating Opera and End of the Road.

7   SCHOLES, ROBERT. "Metafiction." Iowa Review, 1 (Fall),
     100-115.
       Scholes makes a four-fold scheme by dividing the condi-
     tions of being into existence and essence; the order of
     fiction into forms and ideas. A further subdivision is
     made of the fiction of forms into forms (romance); exis-
     tence (novel); ideas (allegory); and essence (myth). Four
     dimensions of criticism correspond to the four dimensions
     of fiction: romance (formal); novel (behavioral); myth
     (structural); and allegory (philosophical). Barth's Lost
     in the Funhouse is analyzed in terms of formal criticism.

8   TANNER, TONY. "The American Novelist as Entropologist."
     London Magazine, 12 (October), 5-18.

1970

Barth mentioned as one author (among others) who uses
the word "entropy" in his works. Tanner investigates the
frequency with which the word occurs in recent American
fiction.

9   TATHAM, CAMPBELL. "The Gilesian Monomyth: Some Remarks on
     the Structure of Giles Goat-Boy." Genre, 3 (December),
     364-375.
         Tatham takes Lord Raglan's twenty-two prerequisites asso-
     ciated with legendary figures (The Hero. A Study in Tradi-
     tion, Myth, and Drama) and coordinates each with Giles.
     While this indicates the extent to which Barth relied on
     Raglan, Tatham contends that an understanding of Barth's
     ironies depends on familiarity with Joseph Campbell's re-
     search. The details of Campbell's "nuclear unit of the
     monomyth" are closely paralleled in Giles. The remainder
     of the article shows that Barth is familiar with Campbell's
     The Hero with a Thousand Faces.

10   TILTON, JOHN W. "Giles Goat-Boy: An Interpretation."
     Bucknell Review, 18 (September), 92-119.
         Mentions The Sot-Weed Factor. Analyzes Giles Goat-Boy.
     Believes novel is an advance from The Sot-Weed Factor be-
     cause Giles "coherently fuses a great many of Barth's ideas
     about the nature of man . . . in an absurdly meaningless
     universe." Tilton educes three myths which reveal "inter-
     dependencies" between Giles form and content: The "Hero
     Myth," the "Founder's Hill Myth," the "Boundary Dispute
     Myth." Tilton uses these to show the unity of mythos and
     logos in Giles. Tilton explores Barth's use of analogy of
     nomenclature, the pattern of events, the rites attendant on
     Giles rise, noting the tendencies of Giles to unify polari-
     ties in the course of interpreting man's plight. Tilton
     discovers contemporary allegories among the mythical pat-
     terns and shows the careful interweaving of such elements.

11   WEINBERG, HELEN. The New Novel in America: The Kafkan Mode
     in Contemporary Fiction. Ithaca and London: Cornell
     University Press, pp. 11-12.
         Mentions End of the Road as representative of absurdist
     novels using surreal means to present the victim-hero's
     situation.

WRITINGS ABOUT JOHN BARTH, 1956-1973

1971

1   ALTIERI, CHARLES. "Organic and Humanist Models in Some
    English Bildungsroman." Journal of General Education, 23
    (October), 220-240.
        Gives examples of organic and human models of personal
    development. Organic ideal insists the self must grow to
    full potential with little interference. Humanist model
    demands encounters with other minds. Barth treats the self-
    development problem by identifying the individual and ar-
    tistic creation. Individual creates self in the same way
    he creates art work. Characters suffer from crippling
    self-awareness. Sees spider metaphor in Lost in the Fun-
    house spinning out terms of definition. Poison in their
    creations.

2   BEAN, JOHN C. "John Barth and Festive Comedy: The Failure of
    Imagination in The Sot-Weed Factor." Xavier University
    Studies, 10 (Spring), 3-15.
        Bean compares Barth to Shakespeare and Fielding. Barth
    gives the manner and style of a festive comedy but not the
    spirit. Barth's irony comes in the discrepancy between the
    novel's festive structure and the non-festive world on which
    it is imposed. While Barth follows the festive structure
    which moves from rigidity to chaos to a new order, he fails
    in the festive spirit which values openness to experience,
    submission to multiplicity, willingness to abandon old
    identities for new ones, a movement to new life and re-
    birth, and happy endings. The Sot-Weed Factor exhibits
    rigidity, fear of multiplicity, and commitment to identi-
    ties. Bean feels that Barth's imagination is dissociated
    from the imagination that transforms and forgives. The
    comic novel is reduced to a series of gags.

3   CHURCHILL, THOMAS. "An Interview with Anthony Burgess."
    Malahot Review, 17 (January), 103-127.
        Burgess says Barth is a promising novelist. The Sot-
    Weed Factor is an important novel, but he thinks that Giles
    Goat-Boy is fakery. Allegory and symbolism "shell out too
    easily."

4   FIEDLER, LESLIE A. "John Barth: An Eccentric Genius." In
    The Collected Essays of Leslie Fiedler. (v. 2). New York:
    Stein and Day, pp. 325-330. Also in On Contemporary
    Literature, R. Kostelanetz, ed. New York: Avon Books,
    1964, pp. 238-243. Also in New Leader, 44 (13 February
    1961), 22-24.

Barth has the obtuseness needed to be a "really" American writer. He approaches each of his inevitable publish-
ing failures with awareness. Barth is interested in the
human condition in The Sot-Weed Factor. Even in antiquity
he finds scandal, terror, and disreputable joy. On another
level the book appears to be put together by a historical
scholar. But he finds no historical truths, only absurd-
ity. Anti-historical joke book--but biggest joke is that
Barth has written something closer to "great American novel"
than any other book of the last decade. Comment on sex and
society also about plight of artist in U.S. by one who pre-
fers irony to self-pity.

5 HARPER, HOWARD M., JR. "Trends in Recent American Fiction."
    Contemporary Literature, 12 (Spring), 204-229.
        Lost in the Funhouse less ambitious than Giles but func-
    tions more personally and movingly. This book is a portrait
    of man who is unhappy with qualities of coldness, cerebral-
    ness, cleverness, and self-consciousness. Barth creates
    "profound human dimensions." Narrator's entry to this
    world only through use of technical expertise is a sad com-
    ment on man and civilization.

6 HARRIS, CHARLES B. "The Absurdist Novels of John Barth." In
    Contemporary American Novelists of the Absurd. New Haven:
    College and University Press, pp. 100-120.
        Mentions The Floating Opera and The End of the Road.
    Analysis of The Sot-Weed Factor and Giles Goat-Boy. Dis-
    cusses Barth's contribution to the novel through imitation
    and innovation; also briefly treats his models. Believes
    Barth's "novels become paradigms of or metaphors for the
    absurdity he examines." Both The Sot-Weed Factor and Giles
    Goat-Boy "attempt to order the world around artificial
    values. . . ." Experience rectifies the heroes' faulty
    visions. As heroes, however, both protagonists are serious
    proponents of life and myth in a comic world. Such a world
    is removed "at least twice from the world of 'objective re-
    ality'. . . ." As in Tom Jones there is farce, but through
    farce, Barth ironically suggests the absurdity that consti-
    tutes his main theme.

7 HAUCK, R. B. "These Fruitful Fruitless Odyssyes: John
    Barth." In A Cheerful Nihilism. Bloomington and London:
    Indiana University Press, pp. 201-236.
        Analyzes The Floating Opera, Lost in the Funhouse, The
    End of the Road, The Sot-Weed Factor, and Giles Goat-Boy.
    Focuses on Barth's "comic absurd creation," Barth's recog-
    nition "of the fun to be had revealing the inseparability

of the real and the fictional world." Sees Barth's world
as one based on unreality as well as reality, as much joke
as dilemma. Barth's fun is "creating absurd alternatives
. . . ." Hauck notes the cyclical tendencies of Barth's
stories, his invention of "worlds within worlds, illumi-
nating both story worlds and real worlds." Thus Barth
blends history and myth, his cyclical structures creating
thematic and symbolic ambiguities.

8   KENEDY, R. C. "John Barth." Art International, 15:26–30.
       Analyzes The Sot-Weed Factor, Giles Goat-Boy. Mentions
    The Floating Opera and End of the Road. Sees Barth as a
    deliberate adherent to new style rather than instinctive.
    Ignores human being's capacity for growth. Characters ex-
    ist in "intellectual equivalent of a vacuum." Flaws of
    Giles are noted as literal transformations without sense
    of humor. The Sot-Weed Factor indicates Barth's inferior
    handling of episodes. Purpose of article is to show Barth's
    failure.

9   LEBOWITZ, NAOMI. "The Twentieth Century Novel: Old Wine in
    New Bottles." In Humanism and the Absurd in the Modern
    Novel. Evanston: Northwestern University Press,
    pp. 123–127.
       Lebowitz makes a distinction between parodic humanists
    and absurdists. The former are always committed to human
    personality and character while the latter remain indiffer-
    ent to the psychological demands of others. Barth pays the
    price of decontamination from the world by a "redundant and
    implosive imagination." In The Sot-Weed Factor, literary
    and historical truths are teased but never translated from
    an epistemological problem into a moral one. Readers may
    feel only a bored admiration.

10 LEFF, LEONARD J. "Utopia Reconstructed: Alienation in
    Vonnegut's God Bless You, Mr. Rosewater." Critique,
    12:29–37.
       Barth's The Floating Opera explores the problem of iden-
    tity and the need for relief from dehumanization. Allows
    internal conflicts precedence over external.

11 MERCER, PETER. "The Rhetoric of Giles Goat-Boy." Novel,
    4:147–158.
       Refers briefly to The Sot-Weed Factor; focuses on the
    language of Giles Goat-Boy. Attempts to show how rhetorical
    changes provide form in the novel. Cites narrative devices,
    rhythm, various thematic polarities, which provide a further
    understanding of the generic potentialities of Giles. Finds

a synthesizing movement accomplished through usage of types of language. Notes relationships of myth and allegory within the language framework. Generically terms the novel "ironic," a repudiation of comedy and ridiculing of tragedy.

12 PAULSON, RONALD. "What is Modern in 18th Century Literature?" Studies in 18th Century Culture, 1:75-86.
    Defines "modern" as relevant. Both eighteenth century and twentieth century (1960's) literature have become constitutive of phenomenal life. Structure seen as constricting. Quotes from Barth's End of the Road used to illustrate.

13 SCHULZ, MAX F. "The Unconfirmed Thesis: Kurt Vonnegut, Black Humor, and Contemporary Art." Critique, 12:5-28.
    Barth mentioned briefly as one author whose heroic efforts to write "incredibly omnibus parodies of knowledge" show it to be for all practical purposes impossible. Black Humorist has the additional option of holding a limited number of viewpoints.

14 TANNER, TONY. "What is the Case?" In City of Words: American Fiction 1950-1970. New York: Harper and Row, pp. 230-259.
    Barth is an author who believes that verbal play precedes existence and experience. He departs from Wittgenstein's "the world is all that is the case." For Barth and his characters, there is a whole range of things which are not the case. Tanner thinks that the disinclination to accept anything as fixed and final involves Barth in a formal problem--how can you have a provisional form? How can you have a self if you are a series of roles? In The Floating Opera, Barth shows the despair involved when faced with the void behind all masks. Jacob Horner in End of the Road has a sense of the plural possibilities in both physical and mental spheres. Barth explores the dangers found both in the compulsion to systematize and the inability to cling to any fragment of system. Tanner relates this to Barth. Author's independence from system and form results in sporting on "lexical playgrounds" where signs become more important than their referents. Tanner states that Barth concedes this somewhat in Lost in the Funhouse and The Sot-Weed Factor. Giles Goat-Boy shows even more strongly the multiple possibilities. Tanner is tempted to the idea of a computer-author. Tanner feels that Barth can get hold of no reality by the time he writes Lost in the Funhouse. Here identity has become continuous with articulation. Possibility has become greater and greater, and, in liberating

himself from necessity, Barth has become "astray in possibility."

15 TATHAM, CAMPBELL. "John Barth and the Aesthetics of Artifice." Contemporary Literature, 12 (Winter), 60-73.
    Shows Barth challenging concepts of novel, relationship between artist, artifact, and reader. Clarifies Barth's basic aesthetic and distinguishes it from his contemporaries. The Floating Opera, The Sot-Weed Factor, and Giles Goat-Boy used as illustrations.

1972

1 ADAMS, PHOEBE. Review of Chimera. Atlantic, 230 (October), 135.
    Old tales are too overlaid with "stylistic smart-alecky, . . . women's lib rhetoric and lumps from Rogets' Thesaurus. . . ."

2 ALLEN, BRUCE. Review of Chimera. Library Journal, 97 (August), 2638.
    Ambiguous position on relationship of fiction to reality. Reviewer feels Barth alone may be able to see through cloudy depths of exploration. Must anticipate his future work with excitement.

3 ANON. Review of Chimera. Book List, 69 (15 November), 274.
    Summary of plot. Reworked tales from Arabian Nights and Greek mythology result in a three-part narrative of considerable erudition.

4 ANON. Review of Chimera. Choice, 9 (December), 1288.
    Mentions Lost in the Funhouse, Giles Goat-Boy, and The Sot-Weed Factor. Grasped experimental techniques he was reaching for in earlier novels. "Parodies The Sot-Weed Factor, style of Nabokov and the feminist ideas of Robert Graves."

5 ANON. Review of Chimera. Kirkus Review, 40 (15 July), 813.
    With this novel, Barth approaches his long impending vanishing point. Tight, esoteric loops of subject and form "swallow each other up in a single abstract identity." Sees a heroic aspect to writer braving the impossible with style and humor, but Barth's determination is seen as somehow eccentric.

1972

6   ANON. Review of Chimera. New York Times Book Review,
      3 December, p. 74.
           Short review. Three myths recast. "Mythology shaped as
      fabulation."

7   ANON. "Briefly Noted." New Yorker (30 September), p. 125.
           Review of Chimera. Parodies in a destructive sense.
      Barth cannot improve on original works. Wants to remind
      us they are there.

8   ANON. "Lost in the Barthhouse." Monitor, 64 (20 September),
      10.
           Review of Chimera. Mentions The Sot-Weed Factor, Lost
      in the Funhouse, and The Floating Opera. Sees novel as in-
      trusion by Barth and his subjects into Arabic and Greco-
      Roman lore. "Self-reflexive horseplay." Reviewer waiting
      for Barth to develop gifts displayed in The Floating Opera.

9   BELLAMY, JOE DAVID. "Algebra and Fire." Falcon, 4:5-15.
           Discusses Barth's views of contemporary literature. In-
      terested in formal experimentation. Disavows title of
      Black Humorist. Admires Nabokov, Borges, Beckett, Calvino,
      Hawkes, Gass, Barthelme, Coover and Reed. Discusses writing
      habits. Mentions The Sot-Weed Factor, The Floating Opera,
      Giles Goat-Boy, and End of the Road.

10   _____. "Having It Both Ways." New American Review,
      15:134-150.
           Interview. Barth talks about literary views. Sees ir-
      realism as characteristic of 70's prose fiction. Problem
      to assimilate what's preceded in twentieth century and
      still tell story. Barth not pessimistic about death of the
      novel. Talks about myth, plot, and character in respect to
      Robbe-Grillet's criticism.

11   BRESLIN, JOHN B. "A Prospect of Books." America, 127
      (7 October), 265.
           Notice of publication of Chimera, not a review as such.
      Novel is triptych which mimes Greek legend.

12   BRYANT, JERRY. "The Novel Looks At Itself--Again." Nation,
      215 (18 December), 631.
           Review of Chimera. Mentions The Sot-Weed Factor, Giles
      Goat-Boy, The Floating Opera, and End of the Road. Novel
      is exploration into the possibility of a new type of fic-
      tion. Disappointing. Preoccupied with the process of in-
      vention. Reader can be entertained only so long and learn
      only so much from Barth's Chinese Box; then it becomes

tedious. Barth has not found something new to say about the world, only a new way to say something about saying something about the world.

13   CRINKLEW, D.   "One Low Voice in Wild Company." National Review, 24 (13 October), 1136.
        Review of Chimera. Immensely readable. Fine, randy comedy. The best Barth has produced.

14   HILLIAM, B., S.J.   "Fiction." America, 127 (18 November), 422.
        Review of Chimera. Book for limited audience; many readers would founder. Novel of controlled madness with artist's created world and reality impinging on each other. Comments on amount of raw sex in book.

15   HIRSH, DAVID.   "John Barth's Freedom Road." Mediterranean Review, 2 (Spring), 38-47.
        Analysis of The End of the Road as existential. Novel one of self-consciousness which leads to alienation. Camus quoted. End of the Road marks end of attempt to portray old values and move to new modes where form is subordinate to artist's freedom.

16   LEHMANN-HAUPT.   "Found in the Funhouse." New York Times, 20 September, p. 45.
        Review of Chimera. Mentions Giles Goat-Boy, The Sot-Weed Factor, and Lost in the Funhouse. Key to fun in Chimera is in its sensuality and mythic element. Quotes from Barth on Lost in the Funhouse.

17   MAY, J. R.   "Loss of World in Barth, Pynchon and Vonnegut: The Varieties of Humorous Apocalypse." In Toward a New Earth: Apocalypse in the American Novel. Notre Dame: University of Notre Dame Press, pp. 172-200.
        May feels that black humor as a critical category has been overused. He makes a distinction between black humor and humorous apocalypse. Black humor points out that life is a joke and the only salvation is laughter. Humorous apocalypse is defined as imagined catastrophe that nonethe-less provokes laughter. May examines Barth's End of the Road as an example of apocalyptic novel. The loss of world in this novel is the end of the world of absolutes that Jacob Horner and Joe Morgan live in. The book is more ex-plicit about the reasons for the end than in describing the end.

18   MICHAELS, L.   Review of Chimera. New York Times Book Review, 24 September, p. 35.

1972

Might become uneasy about book's attack on recent
threats to American maleness, but can accommodate as mythic
matter. Work contains the writer's life; his life contains
Chimera; and it contains its writer inside.

19 OLDERMAN, R. M. "The Grail Knight Goes to College." In
Beyond the Wasteland: A Study of the American Novel in the
Nineteen Sixties. New Haven and London: Yale University
Press, pp. 72-93.
In this chapter on Barth, Olderman continues to illus-
trate his contention that the wasteland is a predominant
image in the novels of the sixties. The wasteland has become one vast institution in Barth's Giles Goat-Boy. Giles'
quest for maturity and redemption transforms him from grail
knight to wounded Fisher King. His progress in his quest
provides basic structure for the narrative movement which
is worked out on two levels beyond the overt allegory. It
is on the mythological and psychological levels that Barth
responds to and parodies two of Eliot's indictments against
the wasteland--a psychological failure to unify our sensi-
bilities and a failure to believe in mythology. Olderman
supports his thesis with examples and quotes from the book.

20 PERKINS, BILL. "In One of Three, Barth Seems Not So Parched
and Plucked After All." National Observer, 11
(7 October), 21.
Barth's Chimera seen as desperate attempt to overcome
writer's block, yet affirms it. "It is soaring and clumsy
. . . rich and impoverished . . . majestic and timid. . . ."
Unifying element is Barth and his search for his muse.
Dunyazadiad is Barth's most rewarding creation in years.
Hope for the future.

21 PRESCOTT, P. S. Review of Chimera. Newsweek, 80
(9 October), 108.
Substance of stories become inseparable from narration.
Style is slangy, sexy, yet formal. Ordering of words best
grasped when read aloud.

22 RODRIGUES, EUSEBIO. "The Living Sakhyan in Barth's Giles
Goat-Boy." Notes on Contemporary Literature, 2 (September),
7-8.
Briefs Western readers on significance of Dalai Lama who
fled to India from Tibet in 1959. Mythically he is not the
Buddha but a page who has achieved enlightenment but refused
Nirvana to be a savior to all beings. Shows Giles displays
the fundamental Sakhyan truth that self is an illusion.

46

Writings about John Barth, 1956-1973

23   SALE, ROGER. "Enemies, Foreigners, and Friends." Hudson
        Review, 25 (Winter 1972-73), 702.
            Review of Chimera. Sale is no fan of Barth but read
        first story with pleasure. Best thing since early scenes
        in End of the Road.

24   SHENKER, I. "Complicated Simple Things." New York Times,
        24 September, p. 35.
            Interview. Barth likes to make simple things compli-
        cated. Wants to write splendid stories without turning
        back on history. Barth discusses The Floating Opera, End
        of the Road, The Sot-Weed Factor, and Giles Goat-Boy.

25   SHEPPARED, R. Z. "Scheherazade and Friend." Time, 100
        (2 October), 80.
            Review of Chimera. Mentions The Floating Opera, The
        Sot-Weed Factor, and Giles Goat-Boy. Variation on a number
        of Barth's favorite themes. Scheherazade stories of neces-
        sity: to save neck. Hard to tell who "is muse and bemused."

26   WEIXLMANN, JOSEPH N. "John Barth: A Bibliography."
        Critique, 13:45-56.
            Lists primary sources for novels, short fiction, non-
        fiction, and tapes and discs. Biography, criticism, and
        bibliography.

1973

1   ANON. Review of Chimera. Best Sellers, 33 (1 November), 355.
            Reworking of Scheherazade theme. "Only for the . . .
        literates who are accustomed to mythical sex in abundance
        and crudity."

2   ANON. Review of Chimera. Virginia Quarterly Review, 49
        (Winter), viii.
            Barth's book is again "a cerebral exercise of the highest
        order." "A challenge for the literate and a trap for the
        unwary. . . ." Book is a considerable achievement.

3   BIENSTOCK, BEVERLY G. "Lingering on the Autognostic Verge:
        John Barth's Lost in the Funhouse." Modern Fiction Studies,
        19 (Spring), 69-78.
            Barth's The Floating Opera and The End of the Road deal
        with a persona who reflects his surroundings. In The Sot-
        Weed Factor and Giles Goat-Boy, Bienstock feels that Barth
        becomes caught up with his masquerades and drags the reader
        with him. She sees Lost in the Funhouse as a huge "not

wholly unserious" joke on the reader, an exploration of the printed word. Fiction as an audience participation medium, and a statement of the eternal recurrence Barth sees in the universe. Bienstock asks: Who confirms whose existence? The writer gives immortality to his characters, hoping to reflect back on himself. We read; therefore, we and the author exist. "We go on forever exchanging masks in a fantastic hall of mirrors, and one shouldn't try to tell the dancer from the dance."

4   ELLMANN, MARY. Review of <u>Chimera</u>. <u>The Yale Review</u> (Spring), p. 468.
     Mentions <u>The Sot-Weed Factor</u> and <u>Giles Goat-Boy</u>. Novel aspires to be both mythical and comic. Barth tries to "address the archetypes directly" instead of using them as background. Title is "special pleading for . . . fantasy as fact, art as life, and the like."

5   EWELL, BARBARA C., S.S.N.D. "John Barth: The Artist of History." <u>The Southern Literary Journal</u>, 5 (Spring), 32-46.
     Analyzes <u>The Floating Opera</u>, <u>End of the Road</u>, and <u>The Sot-Weed Factor</u> as novels which reflect Barth's philosophical position that art, innocence, and martyrdom are assertions against the chaos, not only past but of the "whole of the Real." Ewell feels that this belief provides the basis for Barth's technical as well as thematic treatment of the past in <u>The Sot-Weed Factor</u>.

6   HENDIN, J. "John Barth's Fictions for Survival." <u>Harper's Magazine</u>, 247 (September), 102-106.
     Reviews of <u>The End of the Road</u>, <u>The Floating Opera</u>, <u>The Sot-Weed Factor</u>, <u>Lost in the Funhouse</u>, <u>Giles Goat-Boy</u>, and <u>Chimera</u>. Barth's "no-men run back through time to legend, to supreme fictions." Barth makes falling apart in identity crises pure entertainment.

7   HINDEN, MICHAEL. "<u>Lost in the Funhouse</u>: Barth's Use of the Recent Past." <u>20th Century Literature</u>, 19 (April), 107-119.
     Novel reveals "dazzling display of modernist techniques even while it examines the depletion of . . . forms of modernist expression. . . ." Hinden examines Joycean patterns and how the novel defines and exhausts its own possibilities.

8   JONES, D. ALLEN. "The Game of the Name in Barth's <u>The Sot-Weed Factor</u>." <u>Research Studies</u>, 40:219-221.
     Jones relates the many meanings of the name Henry Burlingame III to the novel itself. "Burl" as noun refers to

know, as verb to removal of knots. Each of his identities is like a knot, and the reader's task becomes parallel to his own--the unraveling or "burling" of the search for identity. "Henry," literally "ruler of the preserve," directs the "game." "Game" as lame or injured refers to Burlingame's small member, making him a "game-cock."

9   KAZIN, ALFRED. "The Absurd as a Contemporary Style." In
     Bright Book of Life: American Novelists and Storytellers
     from Hemingway to Mailer. Boston: Little, Brown and
     Company, pp. 280-281.
          Quotes from Barth's End of the Road used as examples to
     illustrate the difference between American and European ab-
     surdists. Unlike Europeans, Americans explain and explain.
     The former have a quarrel with existence, the latter real-
     ized limitations of power. The absurd becomes transmis-
     sible.

10   LE CLAIR, THOMAS. "John Barth's The Floating Opera: Death
     and the Craft of Fiction." Texas Studies in Literature and
     Language, 14 (Winter), 711-730.
          Analyzes The Floating Opera, The Sot-Weed Factor, The
     End of the Road, and Giles Goat-Boy in light of the premise
     that as Barth's fictionalizers shape their lives according
     to Barth's own aesthetic qualities, Barth's form or mode
     becomes a metaphor for his concerns. His characters fic-
     tionalize their lives in an effort to deny the irrationality
     of their experience. They can conceive of a story ending
     but not the storyteller. Barth's heroes have progressively
     more control over the outside world which is reflected in
     the author's own progress toward "baroque artificiality and
     extreme parody." Le Clair sees both heroes and author as
     using art for life's sake. The progressive impotency of
     the characters represents Barth's sacrificial metaphor for
     the price paid in denying identify, sincerity, and
     responsibility.

11   MEYER, ARLIN G. "Form, Fluidity, and Flexibility in Recent
     American Fiction." Cresset, 36 (April), 11-15.
          Review of Tanner's City of Words. Chimera seen as car-
     rying out End of the Road's mythotherapy. "Perseid" dense
     and confusing, cannot distinguish from fiction, myth and
     history. Meyer says, "its all great fun to try."

12   PRESCOTT, P. S. and WALTER CLEMONS. "Readout: The Year in
     Books." Newsweek, 81 (1 January), 53.
          Brief review of Chimera. Slangy, punning prose, "ex-
     trapolating from myth to metaphysical foolery." Stories
     are funny and engaging.

1973

13   SCHULZ, M. F.   "The Metaphysics of Multiplicity; and, The
      Thousand and One Masks of John Barth."   In Black Humor
      Fiction of the Sixties.   Athens: Ohio University Press,
      pp. 17-42.
          Black humorists see life as a maze that is multiple and
      endless.   Quantitative comprehension in their strategy,
      hoping that the wide-angled vision will lead to verbal pat-
      terns meaningful to our experience.   Their aim is to formu-
      late symbols for a metaphysical reality that suggests un-
      bounded multiplicity.   Schulz mentions six techniques used
      to suggest metaphysical multiplicity.   New starts, perennial
      renewal, and ontological insecurity are concerns of Barth.
      What Borges does with place, Barth does with people.   Barth
      maintains the fiction of continuity and the reality of per-
      son in the limited persistence of the word by retelling old
      myths, coming paradigmatically closer to Borges, and lam-
      pooning the anti-Gutenberg cries of McLuhan.   Barth has
      found that parody is the best method.

Jerzy Kosinski

Writings by Jerzy Kosinski

<u>Books</u>

<u>The Future is Ours, Comrade</u>. Garden City, N. Y.: Doubleday, 1960 (published under the pseudonym Joseph Novak). Toronto: Doubleday, 1960. London: Bodley Head, 1960. New York: Dutton, 1964.

<u>No Third Path</u>. Garden City, N. Y.: Doubleday, 1962 (published under the pseudonym Joseph Novak). Toronto: Doubleday, 1962.

<u>The Painted Bird</u>. Boston: Houghton, 1965. Toronto: Thomas Allen, 1966. London: W. H. Allen, 1966. New York: Pocket Books, 1966. London: Congi Books, 1967. New York: Modern Library, 1970. New York: Bantam, 1972.

<u>Notes of the Author on "The Painted Bird."</u> New York: Scientia-Factum, 1965.

<u>Steps</u>. New York: Random House, 1968. London: Bodley Head, 1969. New York: Bantam, 1969. London: Congi Books, 1970.

<u>The Art of the Self: Essays a propos "Steps."</u> New York: Scientia-Factum, 1968.

<u>Being There</u>. New York: Harcourt, 1971. London: Bodley Head, 1971. New York: Bantam, 1972.

<u>The Devil Tree</u>. New York: Harcourt, 1973. New York: Bantam, 1974. [Note: The compilers note the omission of Cockpit

[Note: The compilers note the omission of <u>Cockpit</u> which was published after the completion of their research.]

<u>Articles</u>

"How My Comrades Live." Excerpts from <u>The Future is Ours, Comrade</u>. <u>Saturday Evening Post</u>, 232 (14 May 1960), pp. 23-25.

Writings by Jerzy Kosinski

"Dead Souls on Campus." New York Times, 13 October 1970, p. 4.

"Maxims of Jerzy Kosinski." Confrontation, 3 (Winter/Spring 1970), 75.

"Reality Behind Words." New York Times, 3 October 1971, p. 3.

"The Art of the Self: Essays a propos Steps." Exile, 1 (1972), 48-67.

"Lone Wolf." American Scholar, 42 (Spring 1973), 193-194.

"To Hold A Pen." American Scholar, 42 (Autumn 1973), 555-556.

Writings about
Jerzy Kosinski, 1960-1973

1960

1   ANON. Review of The Future is Ours, Comrade. Booklist, 56
       (1 July), 651.
         An important book that goes beyond first impressions and
       generalizations. The report is remarkably candid and in-
       formative because of author's ability to meet a large and
       varied group of people.

2   BRICKMAN, W. W. Review of The Future is Ours, Comrade.
       School and Society, 88 (17 December), 502.
         Very brief review with one sentence summary of important
       points. Calls the book "illuminating" with the chapter on
       education mentioned particularly.

3   CHAMBERLIN, W. H. "Life in Russia: What It's Like."
       Chicago Sun Tribune, 29 May, p. 2.
         Review of The Future is Ours, Comrade. Presents cramped
       housing, payola, Soviet tourist supervision, secret police,
       interrogation but no impression of seething discontent.
       While the book may not be accurate in this respect, it is
       well worth reading because of Novak's facilities for ob-
       servation.

4   CRANKSHAW, EDWARD. "Reporting on Russia." Observer
       (30 October), p. 22.
         Review of The Future is Ours, Comrade. Criticizes the
       author's deficient sense of humor and ignorance of human
       nature. Praises the book for portraying clearly the me-
       chanics of Soviet society. Despite its shortcomings, the
       book represents a genuine contribution.

5   HARRISON, J. G. "Conversations with the Russians." Christian
       Science Monitor, 25 May, p. 13.
         Reviews The Future is Ours, Comrade. Book should be
       thoughtfully and carefully read for its explication of So-
       viet views. Seen as especially valuable are the parts on

1960

cultural differences and the citizen conviction of Communist economic and military victory.

6   HOTTELET, RICHARD C. "From Collective to Kremlin, it's one Big State of Nerves." New York Times Book Review, 22 May, p. 3.
        Review of The Future is Ours, Comrade. Interesting and fascinating personal document, valuable for the conclusions it allows the reader to draw. Shows the Soviet Union turned from medieval to enlightened despotism without relaxing hold on its subjects.

7   JASKIEVICZ, W. C. Review of The Future is Ours, Comrade. Best Sellers (15 June), p. 113.
        Book is more revealing than most dealing with the same subject. Finds it incredible that so many people should tell so much to one man. Novak shows what Communism has done to man's spirit.

8   JORDEN, WILLIAM J. "Collective Way of Being." New Leader (24 October), pp. 24-25.
        Review of The Future is Ours, Comrade. Author's knowledge of Russian and his ability to establish normal contacts with a variety of people result in one of the best pictures of "the new Soviet man" available. Seen as most valuable is Novak's warning that we must not transfer our standards to a society as different as that of the Soviet Union. Jorden's only criticism is that Novak does not include the Soviet peasant among his "gallery of comrades."

9   KITCHING, JESSIE. Review of The Future is Ours, Comrade. Publisher's Weekly, 177 (18 April), 48.
        Explains origin of book in Novak's extensive visit to Russia. Notes his concentration on "the ordinary Russian life." Finds the book a "sobering but vastly interesting view, of a people drab, chauvinistic, puritannical [sic], and militaristic."

10   LITVINOFF, E. "Several Types of Soviet Reality." Guardian (21 October), p. 8.
        Review of The Future is Ours, Comrade. Book will not fit anyone's preconceptions. Russian people talking with "passion, vigour, intelligence and disconcerting candour." Litvinoff feels they are worth listening to.

11   ROSENFELD, STEPHEN. "Behind the Iron Curtain." Washington Post, 22 May, p. E6.

1962

Review of <u>The Future is Ours, Comrade</u>. One of the best,
revealing, and convincing efforts to tell what the Russian
people are like. Novak's people are compellingly real.

12   RUEF, JOSEPH. Review of <u>The Future is Ours, Comrade</u>. <u>Library
     Journal</u>, 85 (15 April), 1585.
         Finds Novak's personal conversations with Russian people
     interesting, but questions their authenticity. Thinks the
     reports on the "continuous stress toward conformity" to be
     "illuminating (and frightening)" and believes one should not
     read the book uncritically.

13   WERTH, ALEXANDER. "America's Friend or African Missionary?"
     <u>New Statesman</u> (22 October), p. 620.
         <u>The Future is Ours, Comrade</u> is reviewed with three other
     books on the Soviet Union. "Light and readable," much of
     what the book has to say is plausible, some of it improb-
     able. Includes a little bit of everything that Russians
     think about.

1961

1   ANON. "Soviet Sketches." <u>Times Literary Supplement</u>
     (3 February), p. 75.
         Review of <u>The Future is Ours, Comrade</u>. Seen as limita-
     tions are scenes laid in places commonly open to tourists
     and journalists and the lack of conversations with peasants.
     Provides interesting details to familiar questions.

1962

1   ANON. Review of <u>No Third Path</u>. <u>Booklist</u>, 58 (15 April), 551.
         Likes author's use of quotations from Soviet newspapers
     and literature to support the theme of how fear of the col-
     lective deters individualism in all classes. Sees the book
     as an excellent complement to Mehnert's <u>Soviet Man and His
     World</u> because of its different approach.

2   ANON. Review of <u>No Third Path</u>. <u>New Yorker</u> (17 March),
     p. 188.
         Portrayal of self-satisfied society whose goal is to
     subordinate the individual to the collective. Depressing
     but useful, reminds us that if Russians seem different,
     it's because they are.

Writings about Jerzy Kosinski, 1960-1973

1962

3   CHAMBERLIN, W. H.   "First Hand Impressions of how the Soviet
    Mind Works."   Chicago Sunday Tribune, 25 February, p. 4.
        Review of No Third Path.   Further analysis which began
    in The Future is Ours, Comrade.   Book would have gained by
    a more analytical approach by the author, but as a collec-
    tion of raw material of Soviet life and psychology, it is
    one of the best.

4   O'CONNOR, WILLIAM.   Review of No Third Path.   Best Sellers
    (1 March), pp. 479-480.
        Mentions The Future is Ours, Comrade.   Praises No Third
    Path for its "live" presence which makes the reading full
    of discovery.   Recommends that it take a well deserved place
    next to the author's first work.

5   PISKO, ERNEST S.   "A Condition of Super-integration."
    Christian Science Monitor, 13 April, p. 15.
        No Third Path reviewed with Mehnert's Soviet Man and His
    World.   Deeply disturbing story showing how leaders have
    succeeded in replacing individualism with conditioned re-
    flexes.   Pisko sees, in a closer examination of the case
    histories, evidence that Soviets pay protective lip ser-
    vice.   They will find a "third path" someday.

6   ROBERTS, HENRY L.   Review of No Third Path.   Foreign Affairs
    (July), p. 672.
        Mentions The Future is Ours, Comrade.   Presentation of
    Russia and the world as seen from the inside.   Particularly
    good are the sections on collective life.

7   ROSENFELD, STEPHEN S.   "Churchill's Dictum Denied."
    Washington Post, 4 March, p. E6.
        Review of No Third Path.   Contrary to Churchill's dictum
    that Russia is a "riddle wrapped in a mystery inside an
    enigma," Novak knows too much.   Shows perceptive insights
    into organizational and psychic ties that bind individuals
    to collectives.   Rosenfeld feels that Novak used his bright-
    est material in The Future is Ours, Comrade.

8   SPENCER, FOSTER L.   Review of No Third Path.   Springfield
    Republican, 25 February, p. 40.
        Novak presents a socio-psychological study which sheds
    light on the Soviet system and answers the question of why
    the society possesses a militant loyalty and blind faith
    in totalitarianism.

9   SUMMENT, GEORGE.   Review of No Third Path.   Library Journal,
    87 (15 March), 1146-1147.

Praises as source material the recorded conversations
with Soviet people. Feels best chapters are on the system
of collectives. Praises the book as a "sociological case
study," but believes summary and index should be added.

1965

1   ANON. Review of The Painted Bird. Kirkus, 33 (1 August),
      785-786.
          Brief summary of plot. The novel is "purely and simply
      a panoply of horror." Book is not a parable nor symbolic.
      Kosinski is a brilliant writer.

2   BAUKE, JOSEPH P. "No Wakening from Nightmare." Saturday
      Review (13 November), p. 64.
          Review of The Painted Bird. Book proves again that our
      century outdid all others in cruelty towards children. With
      terrifying impact, Kosinski evokes a world of gothic mon-
      strosities. Ring of autobiographical truth lifts the book
      above a modish exercise to shock the reader. Kosinski is a
      "master of the macabre," an authentic voice of the children
      of this century.

3   BUNKER, PATRICIA. Review of The Painted Bird. Saturday
      Review (2 October), p. 49.
          One sentence review and summary of plot. Six-year-old
      refugee boy introduced to "evil and bestiality inherent in
      fear-consumed men."

4   FIELD, ANDREW. "The Butcher's Helpers." Book Week
      (17 October), p. 2.
          Review of The Painted Bird. Field states that no novel
      has delved so deeply into the "Nazi mentality" as this one.
      Book shows that this mentality is not confined to the limits
      of a uniform or nationality. Enlightenment to be gained in
      its "flame-dark pages."

5   HALLEY, ANNE. "Poor Boy Spreads His Wings." Nation, 20
      (29 November), 424.
          Review of The Painted Bird. Sees the novel as belonging
      to two genres: 1) that genre which teaches us that life
      under love and reason is a special dispensation; and 2) the
      fairy-tale genre. The characters are buried deep in our
      consciousness. Anti-fairy-tale in that the folktale motifs
      show a realistic "twist" or reversal in which neither jus-
      tice nor reason prevail. Halley sees in the epilogue a
      strange reversal. The boy learns freedom and independence

1965

    among the peasants and Kosinski implies that America is a
comparable place for man to spread his wings and survive.
The reviewer hopes for a world "less natural," one in which
less heroic methods are needed to survive.

6   IVSKY, OLEG. Review of The Painted Bird. Library Journal, 90
      (1 October), 4109.
          Feels the book is "like a badly abscessed tooth, . . .
impossible to leave alone." Admires its folktale quality
and simplicity. Summarizes plot and highly recommends the
novel to "discriminating readers with castiron stomachs."

7   KITCHING, JESSIE. Review of The Painted Bird. Publisher's
      Weekly, 188 (13 September), 81.
          Summarizes plot and mentions symbolic meaning of "painted
bird." Feels this is "realistic picture of the horrifying
life of thousands of abandoned children in Europe in the
war years."

8   POORE, CHARLES. "Things Like These Happen to People We Know."
      New York Times, 115 (16 October), 25.
          Review of The Painted Bird. Reader's composure is saved
only because Kosinski sets the novel in Eastern Europe. We
can say that it has not happened and is not happening here.
Kosinski is telling us that those who feel injustice do not
necessarily become just and those discriminated against do
not learn tolerance. Poore states that this need not and
cannot be so if civilization is to progress.

9   RYAN, F. L. Review of The Painted Bird. Best Sellers, 25
      (1 November), 299.
          Purely referential nature of the brutalities relieved by
both the symbolic structures which bring us into deeper
levels of meaning and by the autobiographical tone. Kosinski knows that any life is better than death.

10   SCHAPP, DICK. "Stepmother Tongue." Book Week (14 November),
      p. 6.
          Interview with Kosinski who talks about his past and his
work. Of The Painted Bird he says that although the book
is not literal, it is composed of literal incidents, cut
up and rearranged into a pattern. Mentions The Future is
Ours, Comrade and No Third Path. Kosinski states that his
next book will be the first where he is free of himself.

11   WIESEL, ELIE. "Everybody's Victim." New York Times Book
      Review, 31 October, p. 5.

Writings about Jerzy Kosinski, 1960-1973

Review of The Painted Bird. Wiesel states the chronicler has an easier task than the psychologists or sociolo-
gists. He has only to present experience, not explain it.
Most terrifying truths in Painted Bird are: 1) child must
metamorphose into one who hates as it is the only effective
method of survival; and 2) the villagers are ordinary
people. Shows that Auschwitz is more of a concept than a
name. A novel of unusual power and haunting quality.

1966

1 ALLEN, TREVOR. "On Expatriates." Books and Bookmen, 11
   (April), 40.
       Review of The Painted Bird. Mentions The Future is Ours,
   Comrade and No Third Path. Allen has never read a book
   which contained so much "peasant rape, sex lust, sadistic
   brutality, superstition, depravity, evil." He wants more
   testimony before he can believe that the book is anything
   more than a fevered creation of Kosinski's imagination.

2 ANON. Review of The Painted Bird. Booklist, 62 (1 January),
   434.
       Sees the novel as a story of rare and shocking power
   which has the potential to offend those who do not read it
   as "the fable and indictment of man's inhumanity to man
   that it is." Summarizes plot.

3 ANON. Review of The Painted Bird. Choice, 2 (January), 772.
       Very brief review and summary of plot. Novel seen as a
   literary document of World War II. Kosinski's imagery
   "pales Kafkas's."

4 ANON. "Books Received." Times Literary Supplement (19 May),
   p. 461.
       Brief review of The Painted Bird. Style, setting and
   peasants suggest quality of fairy tale. Hansel loses
   Gretel straying into a "nasty part of the twentieth century."

5 COMPTON, NEIL. "Dream of Violence." Commentary, 41 (June),
   92-95.
       Review of The Painted Bird. Compares it to Costillo's
   Child of Our Time and Grass's The Tin Drum. Semi-autobi-
   ographical juxtaposition of innocent childhood and brutal
   adult experience produces "a myth of unrivaled concentration and clarity." Praises Kosinski's highly visual prose
   style but is not sure how novel is to be read. Does not
   take it literally in spite of the "hypnotically convincing"

1966

style and is critical of the implied parallel between the
cultural degradation of the peasants and the political
degradation of Poland. The Red Army episodes also imply
that the world of the villages and the world of politics
exist on the same level. The book is a minor classic not
because it reflects reality but because it portrays "the
dream of violence and alienation" that haunts us all.

6 DAVENPORT, GUY. "Messages from the Lost." National Review,
   18 (8 February), 119.
        The Painted Bird reviewed with Brown's (trsl.) The Prose
   of Osip Mandelstan and Murdoch's The Red and the Green.
   The ostrich reflex is not appropriate as Kosinski's violence is neither prurient nor gratuitous. Novel is elegant
   in its negative definition of humanity. Should be read by
   those who believe the world is civilized. Kosinski shows a
   rare mastery of material.

7 EVANIER, DAVID. Review of The Painted Bird. Commonweal, 84
   (1 July), 422-423.
        Evanier compared novel with Marat Sade and Soul of Wood
   as being deeply moral. Pessimistic reviewer uses excerpts
   to support his thesis that Bird leaves us without hope--
   "the modern condition of our lives."

8 FLEISCHER, LEONORE. Review of The Painted Bird. Publisher's
   Weekly, 190 (12 September), 90.
        Briefly summarizes plot. Finds it a "harrowing, deeply
   moving novel," which describes, "generally, the underside
   of human nature."

9 KAMM, HENRY. "Poles are Bitter About Novel Published Abroad."
   New York Times, 12 December, p. 2.
        Kosinski's The Painted Bird, while not available in
   Polish, is causing a furor in Polish press and magazines.
   They see the novel as part of a general plot of Germans and
   Zionist groups to prepare America psychologically for an
   armed showdown with the Poles and Communist Eastern Europe.

10 PETERSEN, C. "Missing the Boat." Books Today (20 November),
   p. 9.
        Brief review of The Painted Bird. Synopsis of plot,
   calls the novel "powerful, poignant story." Mentions that
   the original reviews were "extra good."

11 WARDLE, IRVING. "New Novels." National Observer (6 March),
   p. 26.
        Review of The Painted Bird. Wardle feels that it is
   relevant to know whether the novel has any foundation in

fact. The prose has the "deadpan clarity of an observing
child" as the book shows narrator evolving from helpless
outcast to self-reliant animal. Kosinski draws a parallel
between human brutalities and the natural order. Pathetic
fallacy has a distancing effect.

12 WILLIAMS, DAVID. "Childhood's End." Punch, 250 (23 March),
    432.
      The Painted Bird reviewed with De'Ath's Just Me and No-
body Else. Boy's experiences cast spell over the reader.
Novel is "brilliant, Hieronymus Bosch-like, allegorical
epitome of all those doomed, anonymous childhoods of the
Nazi era."

1967

1 ASCHERSON, NEAL. "Chronicles of the Holocaust." New York
    Review of Books, 19 (1 June), 23, 25.
      Ascherson describes Treblinka by Steiner and The Painted
Bird as two novels which are suspect. Kosinski's is even
more suspect and uncomfortable as his ability is greater
than Steiner's. Novel is fiction in that Kosinski concen-
trates every imaginable evil into the life of one child.
Reviewer objects to the use of the first person and effect
of recalled experience. Net result for him is that Kosinski's "documentary" is "suspect documentary" and a "dubious
novel."

2 COLES, ROBERT. Review of The Painted Bird. Harvard
    Educational Review, 37 (Summer), 493-496.
      Mentions The Future is Ours, Comrade and No Third Path.
Sensitive review begins with a global listing of man's recent inhumanities to man. Coles sees the novel as a child
speaking to those of us who still murder and torment children. He mentions Vautrin's L'Obsevsteur en Pologne as
support for Kosinski's experiences in Poland. The most
brilliant characteristic of the book is that it only slowly
confronts the reader with the full dimensions of evil.
Coles found it paradoxical that as he read through the book,
he became increasingly speculative and analytical. Both
qualities have little to do with the boy's survival. Coles
mentions that the paperback edition is superior to the original hard cover in that Kosinski has deleted the political
sermonizing at the end. Coles feels that Joseph Novak
should not intrude on Jerzy Kosinski.

Writings about Jerzy Kosinski, 1960-1973

1967

3   MILES, WILLIAM. "Words." <u>Library Journal</u>, 92 (15 June),
     2384.
       Reviews <u>Selected Readings from The Painted Bird</u>. De-
     scribes the nightmarish quality of the novel, indicating
     that the passages chosen to be read by Kosinski picture
     "the cruel and completely bestial nature of humanity as
     seen through the eyes of the six-year-old narrator." Be-
     lieves the readings are "on the whole excellent" but feels
     a small defect relates to Kosinski's occasional mispronun-
     ciation and slurring of words. Still, the reviewer recom-
     mends the readings, "particularly for those record listen-
     ers with strong stomachs."

4   ZELDIS, CHAYYM. "Job, the Child." <u>Jewish Frontier</u>, 24
     (March), 22-26.
       Review of <u>The Painted Bird</u>. Zeldis believes that it
     should be required reading in all high schools. To under-
     stand and be moved by this novel defines the reader as
     civilized. Story is one of force and intensity. Kosinski's
     spare style is unconscious of itself. Serves as nerve-
     tissue to events observed and recalled. Expresses the tri-
     umph of spirit over bestiality. Evil counterbalanced by
     the "human music of the author's soul." The literary and
     the human are inseparable. Story stays with us and grows--
     becomes part of the definition of our human nature.

1968

1   ANON. Review of <u>The Painted Bird</u> and <u>Selected Readings from</u>
     <u>The Painted Bird</u>. <u>Reader's Adviser to the Best in</u>
     <u>Literature</u>. New York and London: Bowker, p. 796.
       Calls both excellent, recommended for those with strong
     stomachs. Short biography of Kosinski with summary of
     plot. Mentions that the book was condemned in Poland.

2   ANON. Review of <u>Steps</u>. <u>Kirkus</u>, 36 (15 August), 927.
       Mentions <u>The Painted Bird</u>. While Kosinski's intention
     was apparent in <u>Bird</u>, he fails with <u>Steps</u>. Although it has
     much in common with the experimental new fiction, <u>Steps</u>
     does not impose substance on "a slipstream of sensation and
     movement."

3   ANON. "Bird of Prey." <u>Time</u> (18 October), p. 114.
       Review of <u>Steps</u>. Book might be read as the consequences
     of a childhood as portrayed in <u>The Painted Bird</u>. The al-
     most autistic state of mind and of prose voice is similar
     in both works. Obsessions in <u>Steps</u> are more horrible

because they lack passion and spontaneity. Hero's control becomes indistinguishable from the books. Unlike Bird, Steps lacks the "grounding situation, the structure and connective tissue" that could have made it more than an expression of a pathological state of mind.

4   BANNON, BARBARA A. Review of Steps. Publisher's Weekly, 194 (5 August), 54.
      Comments on the novel's form, explaining that the title indicates that the reader may follow his own "steps" to find the organizational pattern of an apparently disconnected novel. But readers must be "willing to work hard to achieve an understanding of the work."

5   BLUMENFELD, F. Y. "Dark Dreams." Newsweek, 72 (21 October), 104.
      Review of Steps. Painted Bird and Steps are tools to shock reader into self-awareness. Horror compounded by detachment. Blumenfeld asks if it is the "genuine horror of Goya or the pretense of a Dali." Steps indicates a revolt against the physical limitation of man and the limitations of human behavior. Reviewer senses that Kosinski would like to transgress both. Kosinski's casual approach might make reader wonder if Steps can be seen as leaps of self-indulgence or fantasies rehearsed while lying on a couch.

6   COOK, BRUCE. "The Real McCoy." National Observer, 7 (28 October), 21.
      Review of Steps. Mentions The Future is Ours, Comrade and No Third Path. Also The Painted Bird. Content of Steps is "pure existential pessimism" and violence that are associated with Sartre. But the tone, style, and fundamental voice in the prose are new. "A real writer."

7   CURLEY, ARTHUR. Review of Steps. Library Journal, 93 (15 September), 3156-3157.
      Refers to The Painted Bird. Believes Steps is a continuation of Kosinski's "study of evil" begun in Bird. Describes the structure of Steps as episodic and connected only by fragments of autobiography. Feels it will not have the wide appeal of Bird. It lacks "the central symbol of human endurance . . . which surmounted the horrors in the earlier novel." Praises Steps for its experimentation, its structural sophistication, its "surrealistic study of absurdity rather than of morality."

8   FREMONT-SMITH, ELIOT. "Log of Atrocities." New York Times, 21 October, p. 45.

1968

> Review of Steps. Mentions The Future is Ours, Comrade,
> No Third Path, and The Painted Bird. Steps seen as sequel
> to Bird, not in terms of locale or plot but in terms of a
> theory of human potential. Non-selective cruelty suffered
> by the boy is mirrored in the moral abstraction of the man.
> Powerful in its gratuitous brutality. Allows us to imagine
> a territory where factors which determine moral qualifica-
> tions do not exist. Possibility of having no choice es-
> tablished.

9   HICKS, GRANVILLE. "Sadism and Light Hearts." Saturday Review
    (19 October), pp. 29-30.
>   Review of Steps. Mentions The Painted Bird. Steps is
> more frightening than Bird because it suggests a complete
> collapse of human values. Anonymous narrator of Steps
> might be boy who survived outrageous cruelty of Bird. Both
> characters learn to savor revenge. Kosinski's world is one
> in which anything is permitted and nothing is much fun.

10 JACKSON, KATHERINE GAUSS. "Books in Brief." Harper's, 237
    (November), 160.
>   Review of Steps. Mentions The Painted Bird. Cannot
> quite make sense of the title and wonders where the steps
> lead one. Feels, however, that the "anecdotes" or episodes
> of the novel are effective as experience and that this
> comes from the omnipresence of the narrator.

11 KAUFFMAN, STANLEY. "Out of the Fires." New Republic, 159
    (26 October), 22.
>   Review of Steps, brief comparison with Painted Bird.
> Kauffman states that Steps is derived from the world of
> Bird and is further related by the mosaic method. Steps
> is superior to Bird, more subtly conceived. Some of the
> episodes suggest Babel, Dinesen, and DeMaupassant. Steps
> compared to Ravicz's Blood From the Sky. Both novels con-
> centrate on the male organ as fact and as symbol. Kauffman
> theorizes that the circumsized penis meant death for many
> Jews. For the survivors it certified triumph and its use
> reaffirmed life. Kauffman felt that in Bird Kosinski had
> pulled free of the past. Steps shows that the past is
> still part of his present. Steps does not signify pro-
> gress, only steps taken to accommodate experience and re-
> ality to survive. Only criticism is that a few of the
> episodes seem contrived.

12 KENNER, HUGH. "Keys on a Ring." New York Times Book Review,
    20 October, p. 5.

Writings about Jerzy Kosinski, 1960-1973

Review of Steps. Novel seen as being composed of cirles.
Narrator's recollections imply sequence but no beginning.
His memories imply three categories: cruelty, ritual, and
restless love. Another circle. Prose is "low keyed, ef-
ficient, controlled," encompasses the "banal, the pictur-
esque, the monstrous with never a flicker of surprise."
Kosinski compared to Celine and Kafka. With Kosinski, we
are detained "with a consciousness for which the world of
The Trial and Journey to the End of Night seems a tranquil
norm."

13   McALEER, J. J. Review of Steps. Best Sellers, 28
     (1 November), 316.
         While Steps is sordid, it is too beautiful and reflective
     to shun. Kosinski shows the existential treadmill with his
     chaste style and simple narration. Life is the pursuit of
     awareness, best approached through the intimacies of sex.

14   TUCKER, MARTIN. "A Moralist's Journey Into the Heart of
     Darkness." Commonweal, 89 (29 November), 319-320.
         Complimentary review of Steps. Mentions The Painted
     Bird. Tucker quotes and summarizes to show that Steps is
     about identity denial and power. Praises Kosinski's style
     and brilliant ordering of material. Compares him to Conrad
     as one who shows that "man is whatever he can be; only he
     can be much more than he is." Steps is more impressive
     than Bird; Tucker feels that in Kosinski's first book he
     relied on exotic details and a pat conclusion.

15   WEST, PAUL. "Portrait of a Man Mooning." Book World
     (3 November), p. 18.
         Review of Steps. Mentions The Painted Bird. Pattern of
     of an escape from gloom to light and self-renewal. But the
     impact is one of marking time. Prose style is one of "in-
     explicable flatness." Power and intensity of Bird missing
     here.

16   WOLFF, GEOFFREY. "Growing Poisonous Flowers." New Leader,
     51 (7 October), 18-19.
         Review of Steps. Mentions Painted Bird. Wolff's judg-
     ment of Steps as immoral is confused by his appreciation of
     Kosinski's talent. While Bird also abounds in cruelty and
     perversion, it suggests aberrations that are recognizably
     human. It has resonance and looks to archetypes. Wolff
     sees no symbolic life, no similar resonance in Steps. He
     repeatedly asks why Kosinski wrote the novel. Has high
     praise for author's power and talent but questions their
     use. Sees a fragile barrier between psychosis and esthe-
     tics.

1969

1969

1 ANON. "Album from Auschwitz." Times Literary Supplement
(8 May), p. 481.
Review of Steps. Sometimes Kosinski writes like Camus,
but more often sounds like Polanski. Nothing to criticize
as Kosinski keeps inventiveness and indifference. "Canapé-
tray of the absurd."

2 ANON. "England's Loss." The Times (London), 6 May, p. 10.
Short biography and interview with Kosinski. Kosinski
feels more articulate in English, and he appreciates its
elasticity. Consciously moving to a no-style, style.

3 BAILEY, PAUL. "'Stuff' and Nonsense." London Magazine, 9
(May), 108-112.
Steps one of three novels reviewed. Sex for all tastes;
those who masturbate or do it with mirrors will enjoy this
novel. Bailey feels the unnamed land should be called
Kinkytania. "Ordinary piece of sub-Kafka" which doesn't
hang together. Only redeeming factor is that it gave
American reviewers a chance to drop a few names.

4 BAKER, ROGER. "Off-Beat Ideas." Books and Bookmen (July),
pp. 41-42.
Review of Steps. Book that works like a film. Series
of brief, highly potent scenes, seemingly unconnected episodes; however, internal rhythms work and a pattern emerges.
Kosinski writes with bare-boned precision. Baker disagrees
that the narrator is one who seeks to liberate himself from
convention and morality. Sees him rather as one who is at
the mercy of convention and morality. It is a "brilliant,
cold, unpleasant book."

5 CAPITANCHIK, MAURICE. "Private Lives." Spectator, 222
(9 May), 620.
Review of Steps. Novel is the dream of one who, in
stripping the human mask off of its hypocrisy, disposes of
its features. The hero is all the worse for having been
created by a man of verbal talent.

6 COOLEY, MARGARET. "National Book Awards--The Winners."
Library Journal, 94 (1 April), 1476-1477.
Steps wins a National Book Award for 1968. Also mentions
The Future is Ours, Comrade and No Third Path. Provides
praise for brief vita of Kosinski. Centers on his acceptance address. Kosinski comments on his American experience
and notes the changes which have taken place since he first

came to America. He believes Americans live in a country
now as polarized as Europe; Americans "have become political, and the system responds in turn and invades their
freedom." But Kosinski remarks that his award is signifi-
cant in that here he can publish his work exactly as he
wants; here he can remain himself.

7   FURBANK, P. N. "Fiction's Feelingless Man." The Listener
    (8 May), p. 655.
        Review of Steps. Another example of the late twentieth
    century genre of the "feelingless man." Anything else
    would be absurd in light of concentration camps. Kosinski's
    use of sado-masochistic fantasy as means to discover other
    realities is recently discovered and justified. Episodes
    drop into the mind like stones "with an effect of indiffer-
    ence like the hero's own."

8   HILL, W. B. Review of Steps. America, 120 (3 May), 538.
        Hill sees the steps leading to one man's identification
    with new life in a strange nation. Sense of detail is
    good, but "too many steps."

9   _____. Review of Steps. Choice, 5 (February), 1582.
        Mentions The Painted Bird. Imagery is more intense and
    horrible than in Bird. Kosinski's craft compared to Mel-
    ville and Kafka. These authors enable the reader to ac-
    cept "bitter pill of humanity."

10 HOWE, IRVING. "From the Other Side of the Moon." Harper's,
    238 (March), 102-105.
        Review of Steps. Mentions The Painted Bird. While Howe
    praises Kosinski's style and experimental work, he does not
    fully grasp the meaning. Criticizes Painted Bird for a
    surplus of brutality. Steps more free of expressionistic
    detail. Notices two paradoxes in novel: 1) while Kosinski
    claims no plot in the Aristotelian sense, each incident may
    be viewed as the "plot of a plot"; and 2) arouses an anxiety
    for the re-establishment of traditional order in spite of
    its lack of individual psychology and precise denotations.
    Structural problem with inner relation of parts. Critical
    of the immorality of the spectator whose detachment is
    "from the other side of the moon." Howe would like to find
    the steps to return to a world where men can again have
    names.

11 JONES, D. A. N. "Lean Creatures." New York Review of Books,
    12 (27 February), 16.

1969

> Review of Steps. Kosinski's characters use words for
> what they immediately mean, free from irony and allusions.
> Jones is refreshed by this austerity in comparison with
> other authors. Simplicity especially appropriate for nar-
> rator's main concern, the relation between planning and
> spontaneity in life. Takes one passage, counts the syl-
> lables, and sets it to verse.

12 JONES, RICHARD. "Patterns of Obsession." The Times (London),
   10 May, p. 21.
   Review of Steps. Mentions The Painted Bird. Feels that
   Kosinski never missed a chance to touch up violent details
   in Bird, thus showing a personal obsession. Steps less immediately revolting but suggests that Kosinski, though
   powerful, has a twisted vision. Admires Kosinski's mastery,
   but total effect that of convoluted negativity.

13 JORDAN, CLIVE. "Big 70." New Statesman, 77 (9 May), 665.
   Review of Steps. Jordan sees no logical progression in
   episodes; narrative unity apparent only in narrator's per-
   sonality and autobiographical tone. Book assumes random
   but not anti-human malignity. Jordan sees pity in the
   characters' actions and desires.

14 MUDRICK, MARVIN. "Must We Burn Mmd. de Beauvoir?" The
   Hudson Review, 21 (Winter 1968/69), 751-763.
   Review of Steps and The Painted Bird. While Kosinski
   presents the horrors of his childhood and proves universal
   guilt, he keeps his eyes on the audience. Novels read
   "like slick and cynically selected anthologies." Kosinski
   tries our souls, but they recover quickly.

15 O'MALLEY, MICHAEL. Review of Steps. Critic, 27 (April), 76.
   Novel places essential truth of life in man's wants and
   compulsions. Well-written episodes told by "priest of
   cruelty." O'Malley states that "whole ideas . . . come
   from whole men" and only the "saints of depravity" not
   "dirty little boys" can tell us how it is. This book
   doesn't.

16 RAYMONT, HENRY. "National Book Wards: The Winners."
   New York Times, 11 March, p. 2.
   Kosinski received award for fiction, Steps. Raymont
   sees theme as violence and repression in Poland, and pain
   of adjustment to U. S. technology.

17 ____. "Writer Fearful of Nuclear Peril." New York Times,
   13 March, p. 44.

Writings about Jerzy Kosinski, 1960-1973

Kosinski's speech made at 20th Annual Book Awards sponsored by National Book Committee. Raymont says Kosinski won fiction award for Steps, "a collection of short stories." Mentions Kosinski's comments in acceptance speech. America changed in 12 years. People polarized, violent, wresting freedom from one another. State responds by invading their freedom.

18   STARK, IRVIN. "The Agonies of Survival." Hadassah Magazine (May), pp. 19-20.
    Review of Steps. Mentions The Painted Bird. More document than novel. Kosinski seen as adult who lived through Bird, hence his preoccupation with the physical and amoral. Narrative is deliberately apathetic but fails because expectation of reader to fill in gaps of emotion and value is too much.

19   VONDALER, JOHN KENT. "An Introduction to Jerzy Kosinski's Steps." Language and Literature, pp. 43-49.
    Criticizes jacket cover. Sees steps as leading not up or down but outward from author to reader. Book an exercise in control. Kosinski influenced by World War II. View of life sees only two passions, sexual and mortal. Reader has to give Steps a direction and aim.

1970

1   CENTING, RICHARD. "Jerzy Kosinski." Under The Sign of Pisces; Anais Nin and Her Circle, 1 (Winter), 9-11.
    Centing refers to Nin's discussion of The Painted Bird in Novel of the Future. Mentions Steps, The Art of Self, Essays a' Propos Steps, Notes of the Author on The Painted Bird as being similar to Nin's pamphlets. Some comments by Kosinski about Nin. Both are cultural transplants.

1971

1   ALDRIDGE, JOHN W. "Chance Encounters." Times Literary Supplement (11 June), p. 667.
    Review of Being There. Book does the job of cautionary documentary. Demonstrates the danger of taking the medium's message as a version of experience. Praises Koskinski's subtle, downbeat humor and his skill in providing a hero who is "simple without . . . becoming winsome, whose strength lies . . . in weakness, and whose victory is sweeter for being completely undetected."

1971

2 _____. "The Fabrication of a Culture Hero." Saturday Review,
54 (24 April), 25-27.
Review of Being There. Mentions The Painted Bird and
Steps. Kosinski's works cannot be understood in isolation
from Hawkes, Barthelme, Barth, Sarroute, Robbe-Grillet,
Golding and Grass. But he differs in that his vision is
primarily philosophical. Belongs to tradition of classic
European modernism--Kafka, Camus, Sartre and Dostoevsky.
Ideas are as important as physical sensations. American
novels concerned with raw physical sensations hardly ever
redeemed by ideas. Kosinski free of grass roots anti-in-
tellectualism. Sees The Painted Bird as a parable of de-
monic totalitarianism. Being There is totalitarianism of
a more subtle sort.

3 AMORY, CLEVELAND. "Trade Winds." Saturday Review (17 April),
pp. 16-17.
Casual interview in Kosinski's New York apartment. Discusses childhood, father, studies in Russia and his need
for privacy. Novels are autobiographical, but of his future not his past. Twentieth century is one of totalitarianism. This is the first time there has been a perfect
match between "crude political ideas" and the complex technology that makes them acceptable. Only way to survive is
to serve one's self.

4 ANON. Review of Being There. Booklist, 67 (15 June), 854.
Summary of plot. Painted Bird was more impressive.
Being There is a more obvious and attentuated parable.

5 ANON. Review of Being There. Choice (June), p. 551.
Mentions Painted Bird, Steps. Being There seen as a
progression to a more original and objective act of imagination. Kosinski's book a continuation of his first two, and
even more important reading.

6 ANON. Review of Being There. Kirkus, 15 (February), 193.
Mentions The Painted Bird and Steps. Novel "rebukes
here, affirms there, and exposes, . . . the styrofoam com-
position of our society."

7 ANON. "The Conscience of the Writer." Publisher's Weekly,
199 (22 March), 26-28.
Kosinski does not specifically address himself to his
works in this seminar which also included Herbert Mitgang,
Kurt Vonnegut and poetess Nikki Giovanni. Kosinski feels
his conscience is something he reflects rather than relates.
His main concern is for the future of the novel, "an

abstract medium" now threatened by television and biography because of their externalization of events. People become passive and lay themselves open to manipulation through their non-participation in imaginative art. As for writers, Kosinski believes they "are politically useful when they are writing." Still, he pessimistically feels "that in the future books will be read by secret societies."

8   BANNON, BARBARA A. Review of Being There. Publisher's Weekly, 199 (15 February), 72-73.
     Mentions The Painted Bird and Steps. Finds Kosinski's complex approach "fascinating and disturbing." Summarizes action of Being There, commenting that Kosinski views his protagonist with "a satirical eye and a not-so-mischievous sense of ambiguity that is quite arresting."

9   BROYARD, ANATOLE. "The High Price of Profundity." New York Times, 21 April, p. 45.
     Review of Being There. Kosinski's symbols are so literal that, instead of extending meaning, they step on heels. "Banality dressed as profundity" on every page. Painted Bird was passionate, Steps perfunctory, and now in Being There Kosinski succumbs to that which he set out to satirize.

10   CURLEY, ARTHUR. "By One Who Possesses Some Deep Secret Knowledge." Library Journal, 96 (1 April), 1289.
     Reviews Being There. Mentions Steps. Summarizes plot of novel. Praises Kosinski as "a brilliant and fascinating writer." Compares him to Borges "in economy, precision, and deceptive simplicity." Believes Kosinski "writes with the cool assurance of one who possesses some deep secret knowledge about all of us."

11   DELANY, PAUL. "Chance Learns How From Television." New York Times Book Review, 25 April, p. 7.
     Review of Being There. Mentions The Future is Ours, Comrade, No Third Path, The Painted Bird, and Steps. Being There is Kosinski's first commitment to an American setting. The hard-edged clarity of style and action, so impressive earlier, now verges on thin caricature. As a satire, the novel fails to convince or convict. Earlier works moved us by changing the mundane into the bizarre. Being There keeps us too firmly tied to reality. Delany hopes that Kosinski's radical energy will again be expressed in a vital form.

1971

12 DEMOS, JOHN T. "New Kosinski Novel." <u>Under the Sign of</u>
    <u>Pisces: Anais Nin and Her Circle</u>, 2 (Summer), 2-3.
        Review of <u>Being There</u>. Remarkable novel, density of
    ideas packed into few pages. "Absolute perfect pitch of
    style." Style is the novel.

13 FARRANT, JAMES. "Fiction." <u>Books and Bookmen</u> (June), p. 35.
        Review of <u>Being There</u>. Summary of plot. Story is not
    so compelling as to be called a fable of the fall. Neither
    parable nor realism because there are bits of both. At
    best reducible to a suspense story.

14 FINN, JAMES. "A Rich Parable." <u>New Republic</u>, 164 (26 June),
    32.
        Review of <u>Being There</u>. Mentions <u>The Painted Bird</u> and
    <u>Steps</u>. The identity questions asked by the novel are not
    original, but reader is directed to general questions out-
    side the novel which have validity. Would think less of
    <u>Being There</u> if Kosinski's prior works not known. Grants
    him "the maximum presumption of intention." <u>Being There</u>
    attempts less than first two novels but approaches them in
    control and finish. Shows Kosinski able to work in differ-
    ent forms and take risks of a different kind.

15 GARDNER, MARILYN. "A Lifelong Nobody and a Would-Be Somebody."
    <u>Christian Science Monitor</u>, 27 May, p. 11.
        Review of <u>Being There</u>. "Two-pronged allegorical indict-
    ment" of the mass-media oriented society. Kosinski shows
    two types of deafness and blindness: that imposed from
    outside and the blinders we put on ourselves. The fable
    may be whimsical, but the implications are not.

16 GARMEL, MARION SIMON. "Is Mr. Kosinski's Hero A Savior
    Without Bluff?" <u>National Observer</u> (17 May), p. 19.
        Review of <u>Being There</u>. Mentions <u>The Painted Bird</u> and
    <u>Steps</u>. Cannot call any of Kosinski's works novels. <u>Bird</u>
    is an autobiographical catalogue; <u>Steps</u> a number of thema-
    tic episodes; and <u>Being There</u> a long short story on the
    order of <u>Ethan Frome</u>. Chance not seen as a parable, speak-
    ing Christ in modern dress. His listeners speak in parables;
    he does not. "Scarifying" in that it shows how people see
    only what they want. The blanker the mind the better. Pro-
    vides a vaster space for people to project their dreams.

17 GLASSBOLD, PETER. "Taking a Bad Chance." <u>Nation</u>, 212
    (31 May), 699-700.
        Review of <u>Being There</u>. Mentions <u>The Painted Bird</u> and
    <u>Steps</u>. <u>Painted Bird</u> seen as one of "the strongest works of

fiction to come out of WWII." Steps unsatisfying but received National Book Award in fiction because of Bird.
Being There is far removed from deeply felt experience and
becomes an unsuccessful modern parable with unclear symbols
and an elusive moral. Kosinski's judgment of American
apathy seems anachronistic.

18 GOGAL, JOHN M. "Kosinski's Chance: McLuhan Age Narcissus."
    Notes on Contemporary Literature, 1:8-10.
        Mythical interpretation on two levels. Adam and Eve and
    Narcissus-Echo. Narcissus figure woven into intricate meta-
    phor that serves as basis for contemporary parable.

19 GOSLING, RAY. "Current Fiction." The Times, 20 May, p. 7.
        Review of Being There. Very funny novel. Avant garde
    and sophisticated. Plausible and crisp prose. Kosinski
    creates a folk hero in a totally different style from the
    1960's.

20 GREENSTONE, MARY ANN. "Jerzy Kosinski: Chronicler of the
    Jewish Experience." Studies in Bibliography and Booklore,
    10 (Winter 1971/72), 53-56.
        Painted Bird and Steps seen as works which recreate in-
    justice and barbarism which have been directed against
    twentieth century Jews. Both works are deeply moral, tes-
    tifying that the past must not be forgotten. Included is
    chronological biography of Kosinski and bibliography.

21 HARPER, H. M. Review of Steps. Contemporary Literature, 12
    (Spring), 213-214.
        Book deserves a large audience for its value as a psy-
    chological and sociological document. Harper sees Steps
    as various progressions on different levels. The main pro-
    gression is from personal and sexual to more impersonal,
    intellectual, and destructive episodes. Odyssey from old
    world to new suggests Kosinski's emigration from Poland and
    also the history of modern Western civilization from Medi-
    terranean to Northern Europe to America. Novel appears
    more limited on second reading. Feels the human range of
    the episodes is not large enough to be the whole truth.

22 HOWE, IRVING. "A Gathering of Good Works." Harper's, 243
    (July), 89.
        Reviews Being There. Mentions The Painted Bird and
    Steps. Labels novel a "literary joke," but criticizes the
    ending as "lame." Novel satirizes "the two dominant styles
    or sources of our culture." These are the paralyzing pre-
    lapsarian innocence of the garden and the paralyzing

post-industrial mindlessness of television. The novel reminds Howe of Nathanael West's A Cool Million, "bland on
the surface but caustic in its depth."

23 KEATS, JONATHAN. "Mannerists." New Statesman, 81 (21 May),
    711.
        Review of Being There. Calls it a "grimly humorous
    novella." Kosinski's humor is not everyone's; laughter
    purging rather than refreshing, but the "chilly irony" is
    good to sober up on.

24 KENNEDY, WILLIAM. "Who Here Doesn't Know How Good Kosinski
    Is?" Look (20 April), p. 12.
        Review of Being There. Mentions The Painted Bird. Also
    Steps. Interview with Kosinski. Kosinski the supreme ar-
    tist of the con, survival in hopeless climates. The con
    begins in first novel and appears in the later ones. Ken-
    nedy finds Kosinski to be a man of great literary integrity.
    Author is also a con, would be the last to suffocate in a
    bomb shelter as he would know where the extra air was kept.
    Conned Poland out of a passport on a pretext. Sees his
    literary antecedents as Camus, DeMaupassant, Kuprin, Sartre
    and Malraux. Hates Kafka. Kosinski opposite of the lin-
    guistic exploders like Joyce and Nabokov. Reduction is his
    key word.

25 KROLL, STEPHEN. "Counter-Alger." Book World (20 May), p. 2.
        Review of Being There. Novel is short, stylized, and
    devastating. Life barren and devoid of human contact. Only
    the imagery is vivid and precise. Mentions The Painted Bird
    and Steps.

26 McALEER, J. J. Review of Being There. Best Sellers, 31
    (1 July), 173.
        Mentions The Painted Bird. Spoof of American Dream of
    success and mock heroic jab at simplistic American mental-
    ity. Waiting for Godot of the 1970's.

27 MAY, DERWENT. "Guiding Forces." Encounter, 37 (August), 68.
        Brief review of Being There. One sentence summary of
    plot. Novel like a "seductively flavored pill of pure
    irony that dissolves smoothly and rapidly." Like the pill,
    it will not affect anyone for long.

28 MIDWOOD, BARTON. Review of Being There. Esquire (October),
    p. 63.
        Mentions The Painted Bird and Steps. Barton gives a
    brief biography of Kosinski. Writer of "austere

consistency," whose novels read like an application for a fellowship. The moral of Being There is indisputable. Problem is that a summary of the plot is better than the novel. Padded with "quasi-realistic stage props and . . . soap-opera dialogue."

29 MINUDRI, REGINA. Review of Being There. Library Journal, 96 (15 September), 2939.
    Summarizes plot. Describes Chauncy Gardiner as "a trip." Kosinski's simply stated satire shows the shallowness of society and its desperate search for answers.

30 MORGAN, EDWIN. "President Chance." The Listener (10 June), p. 760.
    Review of Being There. Kosinski's third work is his best. Spare, witty fable of modern times. Approach is cool without being naggingly controlled. Morgan appreciates a "hero who is illiterate without being uncommunicative, and impotent without being uptight."

31 MORSE, J. M. "Satire-Schmatire." Hudson Review, 24 (Autumn), 539.
    Review of Being There. Novel mocks the corporate culture no less than it mocks itself. It's convincing but "so what?"

32 MOUNT, DOUGLAS N. "Authors and Editors: Jerzy Kosinski." Publisher's Weekly, 199 (26 April), 13-16.
    Mentions The Painted Bird, Steps, Being There; refers to nonfiction written under pseudonym of Joseph Novak. Mount interviews Kosinski and notes that he is "incorporated" and "a lover." Addresses himself particularly to Kosinski's personal style, his "movement," which is "the single-minded struggle to avoid restrictions, limits, regimentation." Kosinski desires formlessness in life; he lives to discover what is in him. His novels are part of the larger "movement" in his life. One of Kosinski's interests is language, and he comments on the new freedom he has found in English. It has given him "a new evocative power." Being a novelist is part of his freedom as, he says, to be one "is the freedom to be the maker of the world. No one else has that freedom."

33 PINE, JOHN C. 199 Ways to Review a Book. Scarecrow Press, Inc.: Metuchen, N. J., p. 239.
    Review of The Painted Bird. Summary of plot. Cannot take boy's experiences literally but conveys child's impressions of man's inhumanity to man. Deeply disturbing book.

Writings about Jerzy Kosinski, 1960-1973

1971

34   PRITCHETT, U. S. "Clowns." <u>New York Review of Books</u>, 16
       (1 July), 15.
          Review of <u>Being There</u>. Kosinski's simple, excellent
       prose carries comedy delicately from scene to scene. "Joke
       does become predictable." Pritchett sees novel as a "tender
       allegory," for which reader can supply his own moral.

35   SCHRAPNEL, NORMAN. "Plain and Fancy." <u>Manchester Guardian</u>
       (5 June), p. 15.
          Review of <u>Being There</u>. Now hero in a reverse parable.
       "Male Alice in Kafkaland."

36   SHEPPARD, R. Z. "Playing it by Eye." <u>Time</u> (26 April), p. 93.
          Review of <u>Being There</u>. Mentions <u>The Painted Bird</u> and
       <u>Steps</u>. Reviewer concentrates mostly on Kosinski's life.
       Chance resembles Voltaire's <u>Candide</u> and Buster Keaton.
       Kosinski's laconic prose and ability to animate a character
       who is no character make the novel more than a heavy-handed
       satiric fairy tale. It reflects the author's concern for
       free will in an advanced industrial society. Sheppard re-
       counts those experiences which are autobiographical. Kosin-
       ski sees his American students as "isolated by a collective
       medium." They live within a familiar totalitarian spectrum.

37   TUCKER, MARTIN. "Leading the Life of Chance." <u>Commonweal</u>,
       94 (7 May), 221-222.
          Review of <u>Being There</u>. Mentions <u>The Painted Bird</u> and
       <u>Steps</u>. Kosinski's works are an attempt to present morality
       as a point of view. Tucker sees the three novels as jour-
       neys. <u>Bird</u> moves from survival to safety; in <u>Steps</u> the
       young man controls his experiences as he moves over an "arch
       of order." Reverse order occurs in <u>Being There</u>; a move from
       safety to reality to removal from reality. Praises Kosin-
       ski's sense of humor and satire. Only reservation about
       the novel is its ending. Reviewer would like to know if
       Chance found his rain-filled garden.

38   UPDIKE, JOHN. Review of <u>Being There</u>. <u>New Yorker</u>, 47
       (25 September), 132-134.
          Mentions <u>Steps</u> and <u>The Painted Bird</u>. Updike sees the
       novel as being like its hero, barely existing. Kosinski's
       symbolic structure rests on a realistic base less substan-
       tial than sand. Novel appeals to laws of probability which
       have never been established.

39   WALL, STEPHEN. "Novels." <u>National Observer</u> (23 May), p. 29.
          Review of <u>Being There</u>. Mentions <u>Steps</u>. Part of the
       novel's ironic wit lies in the way Kosinski develops logic

of Chance's situation. Unlike Steps, Being There gives the impression of proceeding from cunning rather than from compulsion. Reflection of the "uncomprehending impressions of the alien in the electronic village."

40 WAUGH, AUBERON. Review of Being There. Spectator, 226 (22 May), 703.
     Novel is unremarkable except that it is extremely well written. Chance is a product of a highly literate man's imagination. An "enjoyable three hours read."

41 WEDDLE, IAN. "Allegory and Imagination." London Magazine, 11 (October/November), 149.
     Being There reviewed with six other novels. Weddle sees Chance as allegory twice removed. Hawthorne knew that one could make a human being over into an allegorical figure, Kosinski tries to make an allegorical figure into a human being. Irony is not sharp enough.

42 WOLFF, GEOFFREY. "The Life of Chance." Newsweek, 77 (26 April), 94-96.
     Review of Being There. Mentions The Painted Bird and Steps. Novel is "acidulous satire." Allegory which demonstrates the disease of thoughtlessness and oblivion. Kosinski's imagination used as tools of revenge in Bird and Steps. Being There moves more tenderly.

1972

1 ALDRIDGE, JOHN W. The Devil in the Fire. New York: Harper's Magazine Press, pp. 267-273.
     Mentions The Painted Bird, Steps, Notes of the Author, The Art of the Self; focuses on Being There. Is impressed with Kosinski's ability to use ideas in his fiction "as concrete modes of dramatic action." Indicates Kosinski's heritage from Black Humor and the French New Novel, but notes primary philosophical approach. Briefly comments on how Being There renders a powerful idea by form of parable.

2 ANON. Review of The Devil Tree. Library Journal (1 November), p. 3621.
     Novel expresses the dark side of American Dream. Brief summary of plot. Struggle for identity--coming of age in America.

3 BANNON, BARBARA A. Review of The Devil Tree. Publisher's Weekly, 202 (11 December), 33.

1972

Mentions The Painted Bird and Steps. Sees The Devil
Tree as an examination of the American Dream turned nightmare. The hero's life is as empty as himself, as he and
others "confirm the fact of their own extinction." Believes the novel's fragmented form contributes to the total
picture of fragmented people.

4   BOYERS, ROBERT. "Language and Reality in Kosinski's Steps."
     The Centennial Review, 16 (Winter), 41-61.
          Analysis of Steps. Mentions The Painted Bird. By not
     providing factual information, Steps lays the burden of
     participation on the reader. Kosinski's ability to unob-
     trusively remind us of what we already know is a fuction of
     the novel's structure. Style is, in his novels, a moral
     act. We realize that mankind has passed beyond any neces-
     sity for lamentation. He evokes "linguistic betrayals,
     . . . the obsessive individualism that has all but destroyed
     authentic communion among human beings." But while Kosinski
     evokes, he refuses to type or classify. Boyers feels that
     Kosinski's neutrality proves its own vulnerability. The
     objectivity is a mask that hides nothing at all. Finally,
     an awareness dawns that we cannot stand apart from the re-
     ality we examine. Guilt becomes a necessity.

5   CAHILL, D. J. "Jerzy Kosinski: Retreat from Violence."
     Twentieth Century Literature, 18 (April), 121-136.
          Mentions The Future is Ours, Comrade and No Third Path,
     but focuses on The Painted Bird and Steps. Seeks to clarify
     the point of Kosinski's visions in the novels by reference
     to his other works and by examination of internal consis-
     tencies in his novels. The core of meaning in both novels
     proceeds from Kosinski's portrayal of violence. Wreaks
     tragic destruction both collectively and individually, but
     the implication of occurrences in the novels is that the
     "cosmic stranger" (protagonist) may save himself by turning
     toward "control" and "concentration" (Steps).

6   COOKE, MICHAEL. "Recent Fiction." Yale Review, 61 (Summer),
     603.
          Review of Being There. "Slender pseudo-allegory" of the
     superstition that the human ethos is the goal and instrument
     of striving. "Not real enough to be allegorical, . . . not
     inventive enough to be surreal."

7   GARDNER, JOHN. "The Way We Write Now." New York Times Book
     Review, 9 July, pp. 32-33.
          Gardner sees novelists, after a period of cynicism,
     struggling to the heroic. Despair replaced by psychological

survival. Kosinski's style in Steps has an undeniable effect. Kosinski is an author whose business is style, not
morality. Where style is the whole concern, there can be
no real drama. Kosinski's pictures present a "morally
static surface."

8   KANE, JOHN. "Jerzy Kosinski: Interview." Yale Literature
    Review, 141 (August), 12-16.
        Interview using excerpts from Steps, Art of Self, The
    Future is Ours, Comrade, The Painted Bird, No Third Path,
    and Being There to answer interviewer questions. Done in
    collaboration with Kosinski.

9   KLINKOWITZ, JEROME. Review of Being There. Falcon, 4
    (March), 122-125.
        Mentions The Future is Ours, Comrade, The Painted Bird,
    Steps. Being There is a solid metaphor, both in theme and
    form, of the self in modern society. Part of Kosinski's
    genius is that writing in an unfamiliar language, he is
    forced more directly into the role of the artist.

10 LANE, META and JOHN WILLIAMS. "The Narrator of The Painted
    Bird: A Case Study." Renascence, 24 (Summer), 198-206.
        Psychoanalytic/psychological interpretation of The
    Painted Bird. Kosinski's novel has to be read in the con-
    text of R. D. Laing's statement about "our present pervasive
    madness that we call normality, sanity, freedom, [and where]
    all our frames of reference are ambiguous and equivocal."
    Boy's survival seen in terms of the defense mechanisms that
    one develops in times of severe stress. Most persistent im-
    pression is that of extreme detachment. In addition to
    physical or psychosomatic reactions, the boy develops the
    mechanisms of withdrawal, fantasy and introjection. Boy's
    restoration to mental health is seen in terms of three
    therapeutic remedies: catharsis, parental gratification
    of basic needs, and removal of threat are examined.

11 LEMON, LEE T. Review of Being There. Prairie Schooner, 45
    (Winter 1971/72), 396.
        Kosinski's style convinces readers that the implausible
    is plausible. Uses our desire to believe that most critical
    problems can be solved by the "natural man."

12 PLIMPTON, G. A. "Art of Fiction." Paris Review, 14 (Summer),
    183-207.
        Interview with Kosinski. Discusses personal and literary
    philosophy. Would not have written in Poland as language
    had to be used to express particular political situation.

1972

Moved to photography as means of making personal statement.
Darkroom became metaphor for his life. Is _Bird_ fiction?
Kosinski replies that all remembered events are fictions we
create to clarify and shape experience. Trauma is relative
and experience cannot be graded. It depends on how it af-
fects the creative mind. Those who are shocked by materials
in his novels will receive a shock every day. English re-
moves the author from his past. Feels he is a different
person when speaking different languages. Sees his prose
as unobtrusive, transparent, as he wants the reader to be
drawn into incident. Avoids any language which calls attention to itself. Not bothered by different reactions to
his works. Writer prompts vision, does not delineate it.

13   RICHEY, CLARENCE. "_Being There_ and Dasein." _Notes on_
     Contemporary Literature, 2 (September), 13-15.
        Richey contends that Kosinski's novels depict modern
     man's confrontation (futile) with quality of Dasein. Ana-
     lyzes _Bird_, _Steps_, and _Being There_ in this light. Points
     toward a future that is "anti-individual . . . totalitarian."

14   WEALES, GERALD. "_The Painted Bird_ and Other Disguises."
     Hollins Critic, 9 (October), 1-12.
        Weales sees _The Future is Ours, Comrade_ and _No Third_
     Path as preceding Kosinski's fiction both in structure and
     language. Structure is a gathering of parts that never be-
     come a whole. In language he goes for sentiment on material
     that cannot make its own point. In opposition to other
     critics, Weales does not agree on simplicity of Kosinski's
     style. _Bird_ is seen as the most powerful of Kosinski's
     works; difficulty lies in the final sections where the book
     ceases to be dramatic and becomes ideological. Greatest
     weakness is his desire to explain things. Most successful
     when he leaves extra-dramatic implications unspoken. After
     going through all of Kosinski's work, Weales suspects that
     the author, apart, watching, does not see the flock clearly
     himself, and his scariest image may be of himself.

1973

1   ADAMS, PHOEBE. Review of _The Devil Tree_. _Atlantic_, 231
     (March), 107.
        Even if the hero's role is taken as a metaphor for
     American society, "there is a whiff of roast chestnut about
     the scheme."

Writings about Jerzy Kosinski, 1960-1973

2 ALTER, ROBERT. "Review of The Devil Tree." New York Times Book Review, 11 February, pp. 2-3.
Mentions The Painted Bird, Steps and Being There. Bird is either an indictment of humanity or the excesses of a sadistic imagination. Steps was erotic, brutal, deficient in feeling and repetitious. Being There is a sketchy fantasy. Devil Tree illustrates how thinly and abstractly Kosinski conceives of humanity. Alters objects to stylistic and cultural clichés. Most deadly are the clichés drawn from psychotherapy. Not the heir to Kafka and Celine, Kosinski's modernism is the most derivative imaginable.

3 ANDERSON, ELLIOTT. "Stepping Down into Drivel." Book World (4 March), p. 5.
Review of The Devil Tree. Mentions The Painted Bird, Steps and Being There. All four novels have in common the bizarre, fragmentary, unbelievable. Devil Tree also very bad. Pattern arbitrary and as pointless as Jonathan's life.

4 ANON. Review of The Devil Tree. Booklist, 69 (15 March), 672.
Kosinski shows remarkable versatility from work to work. Novel ingenious, more stringently metaphorical than previous books.

5 ANON. Review of The Devil Tree. Choice, 10 (June), 620.
Mentions The Painted Bird, Steps and Being There. Kosinski veers into a fiction of isolated reality connected by "ellipses of ennui or chance." Story a subtly vicious retelling of Yeats' Cahoulain/Conubar confrontation. Whalen comes off as a verbal dullard. Book is unpleasant but valid.

6 ANON. Review of The Devil Tree. Virginia Quarterly Review, 49 (Summer), civ.
Superior talent of author takes conventional lost identity theme and conveys far more than words on a page. Step up from the rut of current fiction.

7 ANON. "All in the Margins." Times Literary Supplement (6 July), 2.
Review of The Devil Tree. Novel reminds reviewer of an excellently crafted sampler coupled with trite proverb. Kosinski wasted upon "poor dull dope" Jonathan Whalen. Reader is entitled to more than a case history.

8 ANON. "Kosinski Named New P.E.N. President." Publisher's Weekly, 203 (21 May), 28.

1973

Mentions Steps and The Devil Tree. On May 10, 1973,
Kosinski became new president of P.E.N. American Center.
He replaced Thomas Fleming. Kosinski expressed his desire
to be a "coordinator . . . who would trigger the energies
of P.E.N. members. 'If I can help P.E.N. free one writer
from one day in prison then my tenure as president will
have been successful,' he stated."

9   ANON. "Paperbacks." National Observer (9 September), p. 33.
        Brief review of Being There. Summarizes plot. Calls
novel "entertaining and memorable short fable" with a
strong East European flavor.

10   BELL, PEARL K. "Sterile Diversions." New Leader, 56
     (19 February), 17.
        Review of The Devil Tree. Kosinski's flaccid prose re-
duces everything to a state of "trivial inertia." Same
technique successful earlier, but compared to The Painted
Bird this novel is a "vacuous put-on" written by a machine.

11   CAHILL, DANIEL J. "The Devil Tree: An Interview with Jerzy
     Kosinski." North American Review, 258 (Spring), 56-66.
        Mentions The Painted Bird, Steps, Being There. Focuses
on the personal and interpersonal meanings of relationships
in The Devil Tree. Particularly elicits comments from
Kosinski on "trust" or lack of it passed on as a heritage
from one generation to another. Kosinski, like Henry James,
believes in the further emergence of individual awareness
as a means to humanization. Devil Tree focuses on this
problem in the lives of Jonathan Whalen and others. Kosinski criticizes various institutions and prevailing attitudes
for their inability to provide youth with the means for personal growth. As Kosinski says, "one cannot embrace heavy
industry as the spiritual origin of one's development."
Kosinski feels Devil Tree has artistic and social value as
a picture of the entrapment of the individual in an oppres-
sive society.

12   COALE, SAMUEL. "Quest for the Elusive Self: The Fiction of
     Jerzy Kosinski." Critique, 14:25-37.
        Refers to The Art of the Self, The Painted Bird, Steps,
Being There. Explores the implications of Kosinski's major
theme: "the nature of the individual consciousness." Compares and contrasts Kosinski with others who have centered
on this: Hawthorne, Melville, Poe, Kafka and others. Finds
The Painted Bird Kosinski's best example and finest achievement artistically. Admires Kosinski's "detailed impressions." More concrete than symbols, they create the self

84

and its world, providing "an elemental sense of primitive and dark reality. . . ."

13 CORWIN, PHILLIP. "Evil Without Roots." Nation, 216 (30 April), 566-568.
     Review of The Devil Tree. Mentions The Painted Bird, Steps and Being There. In Bird Kosinski's philosophical pessimism works because it grows directly from experiences within the novel. Corwin sees the author progressively separating his ideas from his characters. Heavy philosophical ideas do not grow out of the conflicts in Steps, Being There and Devil Tree. Theorizes that Kosinski has succumbed to what he is satirizing. Recent fiction portrays "evil without roots." It is as if Kosinski has tried to transport the consciousness of Nazi-occupied Eastern Europe to America of the 1960's. Urges Kosinski to return to the fertile imagination that produced Bird. Too important a talent to be devoured by commercialism.

14 CUNNINGHAM, VALENTINE. "Autogeddon." The Listener, 89 (28 June), 873.
     Review of The Devil Tree. Slight but not uncompelling tale of youth returned from world wide bumming to inheritance left by Poppa. Cunningham is critical that Kosinski hasn't made up his mind on which side of the fence he wants his fiction. Like the youth, he protests only gently against "the tainting power of money."

15 DAVIS, RUSSELL. "The Ravings of the Rich." National Observer (24 June), p. 33.
     Review of The Devil Tree. Monotonous tone reminiscent of "lobotomised dronings of a psychiatrists couch." Novel fails to distinguish itself from considerable mass of depression literature. Riches do not make the hero's condition more distressing to share or more surprising.

16 DE FEO, RONALD. "Two Disappointments, One Disaster." National Review, 25 (16 March), 322.
     Review of The Devil Tree. Mentions Steps. Reviewer does not reject Kosinski's dark vision of life, but objects to the way it is presented. Author's world is too abstract; violence and sex are mechanical. Kosinski is a "perceptive, intelligent man and a talented writer."

17 _____. Review of The Devil Tree. New Republic, 168 (10 March), 23.
     The power Kosinski showed in his first two novels appears only briefly in Devil Tree. Book for the most part a vacuum.

1973

18   EDWARDS, THOMAS R. "Jonathan, Benny, and Solitude."
     New York Review of Books, 20 (22 March), 29.
          Review of The Devil Tree. If we take the novel straight,
     we find it hard to care about the hero. Read as a novel of
     alienation, it is more interesting. If the point of the
     book is to make a useful comment on the politics and pleas-
     ures of the young, reviewer wishes Kosinski had found a
     better way to make it.

19   FALLOWELL, DUNCAN. Review of Devil Tree. Books and Bookmen,
     18 (September), 89.
          Mentions The Painted Bird and Steps. Kosinski strives
     for and sometimes achieves a simple expressive elegance.
     However, the novel is a creation of a "cynical inanition,"
     "listless malaise," and the treatment of sex is ponderous.
     Metaphysical theorizing is not only a substitute for ex-
     perience but trivial page filling on author's part. Re-
     viewer yearns for a sharp axe to expose the "self-important
     shallowness" which like the metaphorical devil tree with
     its choking roots and branches produces "plastic psychology"
     and "unnecessary psychosis."

20   GARMEL, MARION SIMON. "Perfect Freedom Fails Kosinski's
     Searching Hero." National Observer, 12 (10 March), 23.
          Review of The Devil Tree. Mentions Steps. Kosinski's
     novels are novels of ideas, which pull you along until the
     book abruptly ends and you are left to sort out impressions.
     Kosinski would be an abstractionist in the art world; words
     are forms in which readers find their own truth.

21   HISLOP, ALAN. "Company Men." Saturday Review of the Arts, 1
     (March), 70-71.
          Review of The Devil Tree. Mentions Steps. Kosinski re-
     tains his theme of the relationships between the self and
     the not-self. Prose is remarkable, "terse and hard-edged
     but still supple and fluid." Novel does not make a con-
     vincing case that capitalism is self-destructive. Diffi-
     cult for reviewer to see Whalen's disintegration as symptom-
     atic of the disintegration of the world. Feels there is
     something about American life that he was supposed to be-
     lieve before he could understand. Not wholly integrated
     and leaves reader with a "sense of expectations unful-
     filled."

22   HOWES, VICTOR. "Under the Microscope: A Novel in Bits and
     Pieces." Christian Science Monitor, 25 (April), 9.
          Review of The Devil Tree. Mentions The Painted Bird and
     Steps. Negative review, plot revealed in sarcastic,

humorous dialogue between Howes and his wife. All the
scraps add up to alienation, impersonality, etc.

23   HUTCHINSON, JAMES D.   "Authentic Existence and the Puritan
     Ethic." Denver Quarterly, 7 (Winter), 106-114.
        Review of The Devil Tree. Talks about The Painted Bird,
     Steps and Being There. All novels show effort to attain
     authentic existence. Whalen emerges from protagonists of
     preceding novels. He is a composite but also antithesis
     with more complex mythical underpinnings. Whalen is the
     ultimate descendant of Calvin, victim of the Puritan ethic.
     He does not come of age; he comes apart. Plots revenge.
     Revenge leitmotif seen in earlier works. Perversion be-
     comes freedom, the only act of self-will which is left.
     Mythological illnesses haunt his characters. Of all the
     characters, only Chance will endure. He is not concerned
     with authentic existence.

24   LEMON, LEE T. "The Fiction-Gambler." Prairie Schooner, 47
     (Summer), 183-185.
        Review of The Devil Tree. After the excellence of The
     Painted Bird, Steps and Being There, Kosinski has earned
     the right to one disappointing book. "Characters are too
     exceptional to be significant, the style too slick to in-
     vest them with any symbolic import."

25   McALEER, J. J. Review of The Devil Tree. Best Sellers, 32
     (15 February), 525.
        Mentions Steps and Being There. Kosinski's "painted
     bird" becomes a circling satellite reporting on entire
     range of man's affairs in dehumanizing times. Sex becomes
     sad ritual of masochism.

26   NATHAN, PAUL S. "Multiple Kosinskis." Publisher's Weekly,
     203 (30 April), 48.
        Mentions The Devil Tree. Deals with Kosinski's business
     and literary relationships with his translators. Kosinski's
     interest in this area is exceptional. He often meets abroad
     with his translators, goes over each sentence with them,
     and provides dictionaries of words which are difficult to
     translate. For example, as used in The Devil Tree, to be
     committed means to go to a hospital or asylum, not to be-
     come politically or religiously engaged.

27   PRESCOTT, P. S. "The Basis of Horror." Newsweek, 81
     (19 February), 85-86.
        Review of The Devil Tree. Kosinski's essays and fiction
     all seen as a part to develop and exhibit his not-too-hopeful

philosophy. Novel is difficult and impressive. Prescott warns reader not to be misled by novel's simplicity, unconventional narrative structure, and colorless diction. When and if we grasp Kosinski's purpose, its effect is overwhelming.

28   SKOW, JOHN. "Strike it Rich." Time, 101 (19 February), 88.
     Review of The Devil Tree. Mentions The Painted Bird and Steps. Kosinski does not succeed with his attenuation of the obvious. His repeated use of "grim bits from mother nature" amounts to a "stylistic tic." Bird and Steps are as impressive as Devil Tree is futile. Skow believes that Kosinski has strayed too far from his artistic roots.

29   STADE, GEORGE. "The Realities of Fiction and the Fiction of Reality." Harper's, 246 (May), 90-94.
     Reviews The Devil Tree. Also analyzes The Painted Bird, Steps and Being There. Works out dialectics for each of the novels. The novels generally provide a dialectic "between reality and the fantasies that usurp or evade it." Bird gives "us images for those uncanny moments when the lust and cruelty we evade by repression return to usurp reality." "Each vignette [of Steps] takes us one step further beyond the facade of common sense reality and one step further beyond the agencies of inhibition. . . . Being There . . . is a fantasy of the type exemplified by daydreams rather than by nightmares or hallucinations." As for The Devil Tree it is a story about a man whose "fortune allows him to transform his fantasies into realities." Believes Kosinski has a "weak grip on the multiple unrealities that constitute the world in which at present we live."

30   TAYLOR, MARK. Review of The Devil Tree. Commonweal, 99 (2 November).
     Novel reminds reviewer of Antonioni's Zabriskie Point. Both are failed parables, shopworn, unilluminating false images of the "American nightmare." Like the book, Whalen has no soul to lose. Gains the world at no price to himself.

31   WOLFF, GEOFFREY. Review of The Devil Tree. Book World, 7 (25 March), 3, 10.
     Mentions The Painted Bird, Steps and Being There. Kosinski's contempt for characters in the novel is barely contained by calculated stingy prose. As in his earlier works, Kosinski expects the reader to flesh out the literary

skeleton. Novel shows American society as a poor little
rich boy, upside down.

32   YOUNG, TRACY. "On Jerzy Kosinski." <u>Mademoiselle</u>, 77
        (August), 68, 77.
        Basically Young's reaction to <u>The Painted Bird</u> and <u>Steps</u>
     with brief biography of Kosinski. <u>Steps</u> unfolds like a
     bad trip, but written in old-journalism, impassive style.
     Caught in dreamscape of logic and amorality. Novel which
     shows total freedom leads to a horror show. Have to accept
     the constrictions of right and wrong if we want their
     psychic comfort.

Thomas Pynchon

Writings by Thomas Pynchon

Books

<u>V</u>. Philadelphia: J. B. Lippincott, 1963. London: Jonathan
Cape, 1963. Toronto: McClelland & Stewart, 1963. New York:
Modern Library, 1966.

The Crying of Lot 49. Philadelphia: J. B. Lippincott, 1966.
Toronto: McClelland & Stewart, 1966. London: Jonathan Cape,
1967.

Gravity's Rainbow. New York: Viking, 1973. Toronto:
Macmillan, 1973. London: Jonathan Cape, 1973.

Articles

"Mortality and Mercy in Vienna." Epoch, 9 (Spring, 1959),
195-213.

"Low-lands." New World Writing, 16 (1960), 85-108.

"Entropy." Kenyon Review, 22 (1960), 277-292.

"Under the Rose." Noble Savage, 3 (1960), 223-251.

"The Secret Integration." Saturday Evening Post, 237
(December 19, 1964), 36-37, 39, 42-44, 46-49, 51.

"The World (This One), The Flesh (Mrs. Oedipa Maas), and The
Testament of Pierce Inverarity." Esquire, 64 (December,
1965), 170-173, 296, 298-303.

"The Shrink Flips." Cavalier, 16 (March, 1966), 32-33, 88-92.

"A Journey Into the Mind of Watts." New York Times Magazine
(June 12, 1966), 34-35, 78, 80-82, 84. (non-fiction)

Writings about
Thomas Pynchon, 1963-1975

1963

1   ANON. Review of V. Commentary, 36 (Spring), 258.
        Summarizes the action of the novel. Finds Pynchon's
    humor "strenuous" and mostly unfunny, even "unreadable."
    Notes Pynchon's penchant for caricature, which keeps the
    characters "inanimate." Refers to this as a major theme
    in V, but feels Pynchon fails in this respect because his
    characters are worthless. Advises Pynchon should take
    T. S. Eliot's advice for "practice as a novelist: 'Teach
    us to sit still.'"

2   ANON. "A Myth of Alligators." Time, 81 (15 March), 106.
        Review of V. Comments that the myth is merely a small
    part of a novel that "is built on the plan of an expanding
    universe or of one of those whirling platforms at amusement
    parks."

3   ANON. "Notes on Current Books." Virginia Quarterly Review,
        39 (Summer), xxxviii.
        Review of V. Decries the lack of structure and organi-
    zation, but praises the novel as entertaining. Likes the
    author's manner of advancing himself "as a conscious ec-
    centric." Feels this is "literary refreshment of superior
    order."

4   ANON. "Pieces of What." Times Literary Supplement (London),
        (11 October), p. 813.
        Review of V. Pans V as "not exactly a novel" written
    in "many styles . . . at once." Feels V is more shocking
    than The Decameron, written by an author whose "imagination
    feeds on . . . nauseous themes."

5   ANON. "V for Victory." Newsweek, 61 (1 April), 82-84.
        Review of V. Summarizes action. Praises farce and
    comedy; finds V a tough puzzle, "a spectacular cavalcade of
    Western life in the past 75 years. . . ." Notes Pynchon's
    penchant for "precise information." Likes the combinations

1963

"not only in plot but in mood and sense. . . ." Lauds
Pynchon's "picture of life," a novel of "great originality,
complexity, and breadth."

6   ANON. "Wha." New Yorker, 39 (15 June), 113-114.
        Review of V. Summarizes the plot and comments on the
    meaning of the title. Notes that characters' names suggest
    functions, although the title character's name becomes, to
    some extent, ambiguous and richer in meaning. The reviewer
    praises Pynchon for his "knowledgeable nonsense" and satire,
    but feels the novel "is too long and often drones." Calls
    the book "a welcome oddity--a comic novel whose author does
    not take it seriously enough."

7   DOBBS, KILDARE. Tamarack Review, 28 (Summer), 92-93.
        Contends that Pynchon, like Cervantes, sets out to make
    fun of the romantic novel and ends "by writing the greatest
    romance of them all." Examines V as a satire of contempor-
    ary authors. Sees the theme of V as a romance in which the
    criticism of romance becomes a criticism of life."

8   GAINES, ERVIN J. Library Journal, 88 (15 February), 795-796.
        Review of V. Calls it "a jigsaw puzzle, a running so-
    cial criticism, and a detective story." Thinks the charac-
    ters' names are "outrageous . . . their equally chaotic
    behavior . . . material for a nightmare." Believes this
    novel could be a "giant hoax or a remarkable piece of
    literature." Felt this work may be for readers "with highly
    developed tastes for literature."

9   GENTRY, CURT. "The Quest for the Female Named V." San
    Francisco Chronicle (San Francisco Sunday Chronicle This
    World), 19 May, p. 17.
        Finds V a "mystery-modern Arthurian quest." Theme is
    summed up by Eigenvalue when he compares modern history to
    a rippled fabric in which "we are situated . . . at the
    bottom of a fold," unable to see an overall view of life.
    Speculates V will gain underground reputation like Gaddis,
    Barth and Goodman's novels, "more formulative than formid-
    able."

10 GOLD, ARTHUR R. "Like a Yo-Yo, Spinning Through a Dehumanized
    Age." New York Herald Tribune Books, 21 April, p. 3.
        Defiant disorderliness of approach gives more compre-
    hensive image. Gradually past and present dovetail; sees
    theme as "the inanimate" engulfing people. V is allegori-
    cal. Quest is the query, "Whatever happened to man, in
    this century?"

Writings about Thomas Pynchon, 1963-1975

11 GROS, CHARLES G. Best Sellers, The Semi-Monthly Book Review,
    23 (1 April), 12.
        Book review of V. Comments on Pynchon's ability to cre-
    ate "a sort of lunatic verity." Lauds Pynchon's command
    of English, his credibility and his erudition but decries
    his "verbal sewage," his creation of "an allegorical bed-
    lam." Finds an underlying desolation. Concludes that "the
    nihilistic novel, no matter how cleverly contrived, in the
    final analysis is boring."

12 HARTMAN, CARL. "The Fellowship of the Roles." Contact, 15
    (July), 73-75.
        Review of V. Speaks of its comedy and its "voice."
    Separates it from merely picaresque and grotesque genres;
    finds it "untrustworthy as to what it means and what it
    doesn't." Examines various levels of irony and word
    choices (Pynchon's) which lead the critic to believe that
    the novel has a central conflict of "the inanimate vs. the
    animate." Suggests the reader look to chapter 9 for the
    center of the book. Here is revealed what may well be a
    "mysterious reality lurking somewhere behind things."

13 HASSAN, IHAB. "The Futility Corner." Saturday Review, 46
    (23 March), 44.
        Pynchon's V more eccentric than Bellows, Donleavy, Heller
    and Berger. Compelling knowledge of current nihilism.
    "Book reads like a literary hoax." Studied confusion ex-
    presses both the futility and vitality of human life. Dull,
    mannered, gory, but "a striking new talent, a crazy vision."

14 HOFFMAN, FREDERICK J. "The Questing Comedian: Thomas
    Pynchon's V." Critique, 6 (Winter 1963/64), 174-177.
        Compares V to a group of "comic, grotesque, picaresque"
    novels like Burrough's Naked Lunch. V is a "quest" novel,
    a "search for identity," but "exaggerated so as to become
    futile and ludicrous." Comments on the meaning of 'V' as
    a symbol and the meaning of characters' names. Feels it
    is a "clever novel," but that "it makes fun of the reasons
    why it makes fun of everything else."

15 HYMAN, STANLEY EDGAR. "The Goddess and the Schlemihl." The
    New Leader, 46 (18 March), 22-23. Reprinted in On Con-
    temporary Literature, edited with an introduction by
    Richard Kostelanetz (New York: Avon Books, 1964; expanded
    edition, 1969), 506-510; also reprinted in Standards: A
    Chronical of Books For Our Time (New York: Horizon Press,
    1966), 138-142.

1963

    Reviews V. Mentions the many literary influences, from
Sterne to Nathanael West, which are visible. Praises the
novel for its power, ambition and gusto, especially its
comic invention. Deplores Pynchon's "whimsey." Focuses
on the many meanings of V, commenting on its basic embodi-
ment in "some great female principle."

16 LARNER, JEREMY. "The New Schlemihl." Partisan Review, 30
    (Summer), 273-276.
      Review of V. Focuses on the career of Benny Profane as
a "Schlemihl," defined as one who is "a natural-born bumbler
who invariably messes things up for himself and others."
But Benny is one who can still act if he chooses to do so.
Benny, however, does not, and the reviewer believes "the
author chooses the easy moral. . . ." Larner damns Pynchon
with faint praise: he feels "Pynchon's mistakes will prove
fatal to him," even though he "is a writer of incredible
range and intelligence. . . ."

17 LEVINE, PAUL. "Easterns and Westerns." The Hudson Review,
    16 (Autumn), 455-462.
      Believes V is "the apotheosis of the mid-century Ameri-
can novel. . . ." Thinks it is "new picaresque," with a
political vision which derives from Dos Passos' U. S. A.
Calls V an "evocation of 'phantasmagoric art'. . . ."

18 MEIXNER, JOHN A. "The All-Purpose Quest." The Kenyon Review,
    25 (Autumn), 729-735.
      Review of V. Sets up a dialogue with a young author who
aspires to write a novel like Pynchon's. Uses this as a
vehicle to satirize V. Criticizes V for its "sheer bad
writing" and poor characterization. Finds V mostly boring.

19 NICHOLS, LEWIS. "Author." The New York Times Book Review,
    28 April, p. 8.
      Provides personal notes on Pynchon's life and life-style.
Comments on his instincts for careful research.

20 PLIMPTON, GEORGE. "Mata Hari With A Clockwork Eye Alligator
    In The Sewer." The New York Times Book Review, 21 April,
    p. 5.
      Review of V. Indicates the "picaresque" qualities, as
well as failings, of the novel. Summarizes the two plots
and main characterizations. Likes Pynchon's "vigorous and
imaginative style," his "robust humor," and his "tremendous
reservoir of information. . . ." Calls Pynchon "a young
writer of staggering promise."

Writings about Thomas Pynchon, 1963-1975

21 POIRIER, RICHARD. "Cook's Tour." The New York Review of
Books, 1, No. 2:32.
Review of V. Extensively examines the "cryptographic"
meaning of V. Summarizes the two interwoven plots and
praises Pynchon's comedy. Feels Pynchon displays genius
at times, and "in his debut earns the right to be called
one of the best we now have."

22 POLLACK, VENETIA. "New Fiction." Punch, 245 (13 November),
722-723.
Review of V. Believes this book is "not to be entered
into lightly." Finds the scenes "vivid, the writing com-
pelling" and "mature." Calls V "an original work of great
interest."

23 RICKS, CHRISTOPHER. "Voluminous." New Statesman, 66
(11 October), 492.
Review of V. Finds it "long, quirky and allusive, a
pile of faggoted notions, styles and subjects." Feels much
of it is "learned lumber." Devalues the interchapters because of their lack of authentic detail. But praises the
book because of its virtue of knowing "an enormous lot."
Remarks Pynchon has a "talent for exploiting the fact that
fiction is stranger if possibly truth."

24 ROSS, ALAN. Review of V. London Magazine, n.s. 3
(December), 87.
Finds V a "kind of sick museum of prevailing literary
styles." Opines that Pynchon has "energy without taste,
imagination without discipline, inventiveness without self-
criticism." Believes the "final impression is of wearing
garrulousness."

25 SLATOFF, WALTER. Epoch, 12 (Spring), 255-257.
Review of V. Believes it to be "a book of major importance" that "explores . . . just where we are right now
and how we got there." Summarizes characters and action.
Comments on novel's "energetic surface" as opposed to its
"underlying pessimism." Still, Slatoff feels Pynchon writes
about how people have become "inanimate." Pynchon sees his
characters "as terribly and pathetically human," but "his
writing and vision have a disturbing and difficult to define non-human quality." Slatoff defines this in terms of
"inventiveness" and "fecundity." Pynchon accomplishes both,
but is creative "beyond the realm of mere invention."

26 WOOD, PERCY. "Sophisticated Saga of Benny Profane." Chicago
Tribune, 14 April, p. 4.

1964

> Enthusiastic review of $\underline{V}$. Admires Pynchon's "sophisti-
> cated and worldly" string of words, vivid people, bawdy
> humor, literary pratfalls, and slapstick in syntax. "There
> is something for everyone here, in the screwiest 'literate'
> literary venture in many a day."

1964

1   ANON. "Faulkner Novel Award Given." The New York Times, 3
     (3 February), 25.
     The William Faulkner Foundation selects Pynchon for his
     novel $\underline{V}$ for its 1963 first novel award. This award is
     given to "young members of the university faculty."

2   BLACK, STEPHEN A. "The Claw of the Sea-Puss: James Thurber's
     Sense of Experience." Wisconsin Studies in Contemporary
     Literature, 5:222-236 (222).
     Black only mentions Pynchon once, in relation to Pyn-
     chon's similarity to Thurber.

3   HASSAN, IHAB. "Laughter in the Dark: The New Voice in
     American Fiction." The American Scholar, 33:636-638, 640.
     Pynchon is mentioned as one of the younger novelists
     whose fictions contain "dark laughter . . . , a good deal
     of bitterness, and some madness too." They affirm life
     "under the aspect of comedy" and "respond to the incoher-
     ence of life. . . ." They particularly focus on physical
     distortion by describing "spiritual distortion in our
     time. . . ."

4   HYMAN, STANLEY EDGAR. "The American Adam." The New Leader,
     47 (2 March), 20-21. Reprinted in Standards: A Chronicle
     of Books for Our Time (New York: Horizon Press, 1966),
     pp. 204-208.
     Mentions $\underline{V}$ as the most imaginative new American novel
     about the anti-hero.

5   KOCH, STEPHEN. "Imagination in the Abstract." The Antioch
     Review, 24 (Summer), 253-263.
     Compares and contrasts $\underline{V}$ to Sontag's The Benefactor.
     Finds $\underline{V}$ superior because it is filled with movement and
     life. Pynchon's theme is that the "twentieth-century his-
     tory of the human imagination paralyzed in a self-perpetu-
     ating disease . . . the dream of an abstract felicity that
     is really a slow poison, a deadening opiate of human power."
     Finds Pynchon "a social critic with an indisputable moral
     bias. . . ." Believes Pynchon's "caring" is "the animus
     behind the whole farrago."

1965

1 ANON. "John Barth: An Interview." Wisconsin Studies in
Contemporary Literature, 6, No. 1 (Winter-Spring), 3-14
(14).
Barth on writing. He objects to being part of a new
comic genre. He doesn't agree that "Donleavy and Pynchon
and these other chaps are doing the same thing." He traces
his roots back to Rabelais and Machado.

2 DAVIS, DOUGLAS M. "The New Mood: An Obsession with the
Absurd." National Observer, (15 February), p. 22.
Brief mention of Thomas Pynchon as member of new school
of young writers. Traces form and roots of Black Humorists.
Black Humorists imply we are all demented. The mood is
anger based on nihilism. Examines Purdy, Hawkes, Heller,
Donleavy, Burroughs, Southern and Barth in detail. Notes
Pynchon's penchant for "absurd and farcical names," for
example Benny Profane and Stencil.

3 FRIEDMAN, BRUCE JAY. "Foreword." In Black Humor: A Unique
Anthology Including Works by Pynchon, Knickerbocker,
Donleavy, Purdy, Simmons, Recky, Heller, Barth, Celine,
Albee, Southern. Edited by Bruce Jay Friedman. New York:
Bantam Books, vii-xi.
Introduction to an anthology of the work of thirteen
writers of Black Humor. Defines Black Humor as a tool for
"serious and effective social critics." Stresses the individuality of the writers. Pynchon has "a vision so contemporary it makes your nose bleed." Outlines their similarities: "fading line between fantasy and reality" in
modern world forces novelists "to sail into darker waters
somewhere out beyond satire."

4 _____. "Those Clowns of Conscience." New York Herald
Tribune-Book Week (18 July), p. 237.
Friedman defends his choice of authors in his new an-
thology. Pynchon is one of thirteen representative Black
Humorists. Each is unique. Pynchon is outstanding for
his contemporary vision. Good definition of Black Humor.
Friedman concluded that serious social critics are working
through humor.

5 KOSTELANETZ, RICHARD. "Notes on the American Short Story
Today." Minnesota Review, 5:214-221.
Pynchon is mentioned as one of the post-war writers who
influenced the new short story. Kostelanetz traces the es-
thetic development of the modern short story in three

101

historical stages. He mentions that the story becomes a symbol in Pynchon's "Entropy," in contrast to the major trend of short stories in the 1960's. He discusses themes of American absurd fiction, both long and short, and suggests that Pynchon, unlike other contemporary writers, builds his fiction on sophisticated scientific ideas, $\underline{V}$ and "Entropy" are used as examples.

6   _____. The New American Arts. Edited by Richard Kostelanetz. New York: Horizon Press, pp. 16, 22, 202, 203, 214-217.
       Traces the influence of European "esthetic ideas" on the new American arts. Cites Thomas Pynchon as one of the novelists spawned by "the French idea of absurd literature." Uses Pynchon's $\underline{V}$ as an example of revolutionary works more easily accepted by the young.
       American fiction since 1959 fits into "two distinct patterns": "the absurdity of society" and "the madness of self." Thomas Pynchon's novels are included in the first category. Briefly traces the ancestry of the movement. Sees Pynchon as "easily the most accomplished and original very young American writer today," but does not believe him to be as intellectually gifted as Barth. Incoherence both flaw and chief success. Overstatement and multiple images reinforce "Pynchon's special achievement": "a symbol for metaphysical reality." Points out strengths and weaknesses. Chief strength is a good definition of human absurdity; chief weaknesses are incoherence, "unsuccessful jokes," and superficial characters. Good biographical details. Pynchon a novelist to watch.

7   _____. "The Point Is that Life Doesn't Have Any Point." New York Times Book Review, 70 (6 June), 3.
       Groups Pynchon with Purdy, Barthelme, Koch, Heller and Barth as part of a "large body of absurd fiction." Discussion of the absurd novel and its problems. Singles out Catch-22, $\underline{V}$, and The Sot-Weed Factor for a detailed analysis because of their excellence. Good explanation of symbol $\underline{V}$. Sees Pynchon as obsessed with "the discontinuity of human experience." His special achievement is a symbol for metaphysical reality that suggests unbounded multiplicity.

8   LEWIS, R. W. B. Trials of the World: Essays in American Literature and the Humanistic Tradition. New Haven: Yale University Press, pp. 63, 185, 228-234.
       Includes Pynchon's $\underline{V}$ in a list of works that "comprise the continuing 'anti-face' of the American dream." Influenced by Melville. One of the novelists caught between wrath and laughter in a perspective that makes doomsday a

saturnalia. Close look at V. Finds theme "the mechaniza-
tion of man"--from people to things. Compares Pynchon with
Lawrence.

9 PETERSEN, CLARENCE. "Personal Choices for Personal Pleasure."
Chicago Tribune Books Today (28 February), p. 13.
  Pynchon's V first choice on personal list of favorites.
Didn't understand, but enjoyed because "it is wild and
funny and profane . . . and mystical and scary."

10 PHILLIPS, WILLIAM. "Notes On The New Style." Nation, 201,
No. 8 (20 September), 232.
  Cites Pynchon as "one of the two most original talents."
Notes de-civilization has gone a long way; characters will
have to be invented, not created.

1966

1 ANON. Review of The Crying of Lot 49. America, 114
(14 May), 700.
  Writing has the "density of poetry." Scathing social
satire and fantasy overlay the "symbolic fabric of a positive metaphysic." Two key symbols are a painting and a
hieroglyphic. Compassion is Pynchon's "key to meaning."

2 ANON. Review of The Crying of Lot 49. Kirkus Reviews, 34
(January), 28.
  Too bizarre. Satire too unintelligible. Laments that
"a genuine talent had reduced itself to automated kooki-
ness."

3 ANON. Review of The Crying of Lot 49. Newsweek (2 May),
pp. 104-105.
  Outgrowth of V, same world but seeker and object are
simpler, cleaner, and funnier. "Weirdest and funniest two-
person orgy in modern literature." Leaves any statement on
the meaning of human existence unresolved.

4 ANON. Review of The Crying of Lot 49. Playboy, 13 (April),
25-26.
  Shares V's failures--mysterious quests and ambiguous
symbolism--but lacks its sardonic wit and Black Humor.
"The book is all surface, the product of a keen but clut-
tered intelligence, and painfully devoid of life." The
characters' names are on the level of a college humor
magazine.

1966

5   ANON. "Nosepicking Contests." <u>Time</u>, 87 (6 May), 109.
    <u>V</u> is the masterpiece of the Beat Generation, but "its
    successors have contributed little more than absurdity to
    the novel of the absurd." <u>The Crying of Lot 49</u> is typical
    of the "glossolaliac gibberish." "Nosepicking contest"
    incident describes the genre.

6   BEROLZHEIMER, HOBART F. Review of <u>The Crying of Lot 49</u>.
    <u>Library Journal</u>, 91, No. 6 (15 March), 1447.
    <u>The Crying of Lot 49</u> highly recommended for all academic
    and larger public libraries. Avante-garde satire praised.
    Warns conservative readers may be confused and affronted by
    sexual frankness.

7   DONADIO, STEPHEN. "America, America." <u>Partisan Review</u>, 33
    (Summer), 448-452.
    Enthusiastic review of <u>The Crying of Lot 49</u>. Points out
    intensity, intricate irony, and control. Notes varying
    prose styles. Finds central observation in "that paranoia
    is the last sense of community left us."

8   EDINBOROUGH, ARNOLD. "Random Harvest." <u>Saturday Night</u>, 81
    (August), 25-26.
    Review of <u>The Crying of Lot 49</u>. Labels Pynchon a satiri-
    cal writer without a moral foundation. Lauds his style,
    control, and creativity, but finds the novel a hilarious
    hoax that "leaves one flat at the end."

9   GALLOWAY, DAVID D. <u>The Absurd Hero In American Fiction:
    Updike, Styron, Bellow, Salinger</u>. Austin and London:
    University of Texas Press, p. ix.
    Singles out Pynchon's work as most notable contemporary
    chronicle employing "exciting and perhaps crucial new nar-
    rative techniques." Lists with younger Black Humorists
    whose humor "serves to maintain a crucial balance, to avoid
    the pitfalls of preciousness and chic despair."

10 GOLD, ARTHUR. "A Mad Dash After An Unholy Grail." <u>Book Week</u>
    (24 April), p. 5.
    Negative review of <u>The Crying of Lot 49</u>. "Verbal density
    and theoretical value are not enough to make a good novel."
    The Tristero System fails as a literary system because it
    doesn't organize or sharpen our perception. Reviewer wants
    life from a novel, but finds Pynchon's mileau lacking,
    "inanimate."

Writings about Thomas Pynchon, 1963-1975

11   GRADY, R. F. Review of The Crying of Lot 49. Best Sellers,
      26 (15 May), 76.
          Negative review of The Crying of Lot 49. Explanation of
      title. Brief plot summary. Finds Pynchon's novel confus-
      ing, contrived, and boring.

12   HANDLIN, OSCAR. "Reader's Choice." The Atlantic Monthly, 217
      (May), 125-132 ("Style, Form, and Chaos," pp. 127-128).
          The Crying of Lot 49 "reveals the waste of considerable
      talent." "The effects of hyperbole soon become boring" in
      a novel that depends largely on "shock, outrage and exag-
      geration."

13   HASSAN, IHAB. "The Dial and Recent American Fiction."
      C. E. A. Critic, 29, No. 1:1, 3.
          Analysis of five genres of post-war fiction. Includes
      Pynchon's V with Catch 22, The Ginger Man and Rinehart in
      Love under category labelled "the Slapstick Novel." Defines
      the "Slapstick Novel" as "a cry from the voiceless Id, in-
      dicating all civilization." Notes three strains in current
      fiction, including an apocalyptic sense. Mentions Pynchon
      as an example of a novelist who represents the "violence of
      apocalypse."

14   HAUSDORFF, DON. "Thomas Pynchon's Multiple Absurdities."
      Wisconsin Studies in Contemporary Literature, 7 (August),
      258-269.
          Postulates that the best literary antecedent for V is
      "the well-known philosophical autobiography" The Education
      of Henry Adams. Points out numerous parallels in the sym-
      bolism, historical self-consciousness, and ironic pessimism.
      Disagrees with New Leader review by Stanley Hyman. Finds
      direction and thesis in V. Weakness lies in inconsistency
      in Pynchon's design.

15   HICKS, GRANVILLE. "A Plot Against the Post Office."
      Saturday Review, 49 (30 April), 27-28.
          Glowing review of The Crying of Lot 49. With a "light-
      heartedness and a kind of elegance that are peculiarly his,"
      Pynchon gyrates on his toes through a preposterous central
      idea that leads the reader to "question the rationality of
      human existence." In Pynchon's nonrealistic novel the
      "gyrations are wonderful to watch."

16   HYMAN, STANLEY EDGAR. "The American Adam." In his Standards:
      A Chronicle of Books For Our Time. New York: Horizon
      Press, pp. 204-208.
          Brief reference to V as the most imaginative New Ameri-
      can novel, a picaresque comedy of the anti-hero.

WRITINGS ABOUT THOMAS PYNCHON, 1963-1975

1966

17   _____. "The Goddess and the Schlemiel." In his Standards:
      A Chronicle Of Books For Our Time. New York: Horizon
      Press, pp. 138-142.
           Observes that V represents a new sort of fiction. Dis-
      cusses features of V, "a remarkable novel." Lauds Pynchon's
      "fine mean parody" and "garish fantasy." Sees "whimsy" as
      the least successful feature of V. Reprint of 1963.15.

18   LEHMAN-HAUPT, CHRISTOPHER. "End-of-the-World Machine."
      New York Times, 3 June, p. 37.
           "Pynchon's absurdity is not merely absurd." Larger
      ramifications of symbolism point to ominous despair.
      Joycean overtones in names.

19   MALKIN, M. A. Antiquarian Bookman, 37 (16 May), 2134.
           Brief negative review of The Crying of Lot 49. "Bunch
      of nuts strung together."

20   NELSON, MILTON E., JR. "A Thrust At Truth?" Chicago Tribune
      Books Today, 8 May, p. 5.
           The archetypal quest is the thematic center of Pynchon's
      art. The Crying of Lot 49 is a development of the style
      and form of V, partially a critical self-appraisal. The
      Tristero System is the central object of Oedipa's quest for
      order and harmony. Nelson sees the chaos as an expression
      of the ordering motif of communication. Oedipa affirms the
      human need to perceive, and Pynchon, like Joyce, seeks the
      truth.

21   POIRIER, RICHARD. A World Elsewhere: The Place of Style In
      American Literature. New York: Oxford University Press,
      p. 251.
           Mentions Pynchon as one of the comic-apocalyptic writers
      that Dreiser's work anticipates. "In the works of Thomas
      Pynchon, human beings drift into the category of the in-
      animate."

22   _____. "Embattled Underground." The New York Times Book
      Review, 5 (1 May), 42-43.
           Sees The Crying of Lot 49 as a tryst, "a patriotic la-
      mentation, an elaborate effort not to believe the worst
      about the Republic." Novel contains "one of the best paro-
      dies ever written of Jacobean Drama" and the "perhaps final
      parody of California right-wing organizations." Character
      of Oedipa Maas too small for the large job she is given.
      The major character is really Pynchon, a lone survivor
      "looking through the massed wreckage of his civilization,
      'a salad of despair.'"

23   ROSE, REMINGTON. "At Home With Oedipus Maas." The New
      Republic, 154 (14 May), 39-40.
         Negative review of The Crying of Lot 49. "I would call
      The Crying of Lot 49 a well-executed, mildly nasty, pre-
      tentious collage." The novel is "skimpy, cryptic and
      superficial."

24   ROSENTHAL, RAYMOND. "The Lost Treasure." New Leader, 49
      (23 May), 21.
         Scathing review of The Crying of Lot 49. Fashionable,
      sentimental, over-styled gibberish. "A kind of working
      model of all that is wrong with the contemporary novel."
      "No characters, no emotions, no plot, no style."

25   SHATTUCK, ROGER. "The Crying of Lot 49 by Thomas Pynchon."
      New York Review of Books, 6 (23 June), 24.
         Review of The Crying of Lot 49. "A short crisp after-
      thought," a mixed blessing. Lacks V's texture, but Pynchon
      is commenting on the measuring of coincidence, the possi-
      bility of recurrence in history, and the circularity of
      time. "Maxwell's sorting Demon is the most portentious
      'symbol.'"

26   TRACHTENBERG, STANLEY. "Beyond Initiation: Some Recent
      Novels." The Yale Review, 56 (Autumn), 131-134.
         The Crying of Lot 49 is a parody directed "not only at
      man's absurd situation, but at his frantic efforts to ex-
      tricate himself from it." The satire is more fashionable
      than legitimate because of Pynchon's failure to imagine
      the objects of his satire.

27   WENSBERG, ERIK. "The Crying of Lot 49." Commonweal, 84
      (8 July), 446-448.
         Favorable review of The Crying of Lot 49. Artist's ob-
      session with meaning distinguishes Pynchon from Black Humor-
      ists. The Crying of Lot 49 more moving than V because of
      tenderness and elegaic sense of loss which is new to comic
      fiction. Classifies The Crying of Lot 49 as an American
      voice that "stands in the line of The Great Gatsby in its
      concise attempt to capture the dangerous exaltations, and
      the loneliness of this strange place."

1967

1   ANON. Review of The Crying of Lot 49. Publisher's Weekly,
      191 (13 March), 62.

1967

An amusing satire that "makes for interesting reading
for those who don't feel they must have a plot with a beginning, middle and end."

2 ANON. "Language and Literature." Choice, 3, No. 11 (January),
   1017.
        Review of The Crying of Lot 49. Comments that "Pynchon
   established himself as an important contemporary writer with
   the publication of V. . . ." Concludes that "his new novel
   sacrifices density for narrative swiftness, complexity for
   a clearer articulation of his version of Thoreauvian inde-
   pendence." Good plot synopsis.

3 ANON. "Pick of the Paperbacks." Saturday Review (20 May),
   44-45.
        Review of Richard Kostelanetz's new anthology, 12 From
   the Sixties. Pynchon included in group of "most distinguished American writers who have dissected the uncertain-
   ties of the 1960's." Pynchon continues his "mythic march"
   in The Crying of Lot 49.

4 BUCKEYE, ROBERT. "The Anatomy of the Psychic Novel."
   Critique, 9, No. 1:33-45.
        Groups Pynchon with other writers of "the psychic novel,"
   including Grass, Nabokov, Hawkes and Heller. Defines psychic novel as a blurring of Frye's four categories of fiction. Not Black Humor. Contends Pynchon differs from
   Southern, Friedman and Donleavy. Sees lesson to be learned
   from V is that "reality cannot be anything but multiple and
   uncertain." Explicates the modern novel, including V, in
   terms of an understanding of psychic form.

5 BURROWS, MILES. "Paranoid Quests." New Statesman, 73
   (14 April), 513-514.
        Analyzes The Crying of Lot 49 and draws comparisons with
   Corver's The Origin of the Brunists. Impressed by Pynchon's
   "phantasmagoric luxuriance" and metaphysical implications
   "that there is something underlying mere appearances."
   Finds Pynchon's characters "cartoons" compared to the reality of Corver's.

6 CALLOW, PHILLIP. "All Agog." Books and Bookmen, 12 (June),
   20.
        The story and statement of The Crying of Lot 49 are both
   confusing. Pynchon undoubtedly has something to say in
   this bitter satire, but the necessity to entertain and the
   chaos of the presentation puts the message "under a cloud
   of profundity."

Writings about Thomas Pynchon, 1963-1975

7   GALLOWAY, DAVID. "Milk and Honey." Spectator, 218 (14 April),
    425-426.
         Rates The Crying of Lot 49 a disappointing second novel
    by an important comic talent. Though the mysteries of WASTE
    are "too much like an intellectual parlor trick," still
    "its black (or at least dark-hued) humour more often hits
    than it misses." Succinct plot summary.

8   GUERARD, ALBERT J. "Saul Bellow and the Activists: On 'The
    Adventures of Augie March.'" Southern Review, 111 (July),
    584-596.
         Traces influence of Augie March as a trend-setter for
    novelists espousing activist attitudes. Enlarges Steven-
    son's (Daedalus, Spring 1963) list of activists to include
    Pynchon and others. Pynchon is indebted to Bellow for "an
    assumed freedom to shift back and forth between first per-
    son and third, under clear authorial control" and for
    written letters that blend spoken and written effects.

9   LEHAN, RICHARD. "The American Novel--A Survey of 1966."
    Wisconsin Studies in Contemporary Literature, 8 (Summer),
    437-449.
         Finds The Crying of Lot 49 unsuccessful because it is
    motiveless and insufficiently narrated. The "isolated so-
    lipsistic world" of the novel is justified only by an inar-
    ticulate hero "content to remain within the hole in time."

10 MILLER, JAMES E., JR. Quests Surd and Absurd: Essays in
    American Literature. Chicago and London: University of
    Chicago Press, pp. 15-16, 24-25.
         Pynchon's V is listed as one example of post-World War II
    fiction dominated by "black humor." Pynchon "presents a
    fireworks display of immense talent," but there are too many
    fizzles. In V "excessive length lends to tediousness."

11 PRICE, R. G. G. "New Novels." Punch, 252 (26 April), 618.
         The Crying of Lot 49 is an unsuccessful second novel,
    too free-wheeling. Neither amusing, nor comic. Obvious
    creative energy needs harnessing. Tiresome, "formless
    gush."

12 RITTER, JESSE PAUL, JR. "Fearful Comedy: The Fiction of
    Joseph Heller, Günter Grass, and the Social Surrealist
    Genre." Ph.D. dissertation, University of Arkansas, passim.
         Dissertation analyzing Pynchon's novels within a layer
    context to "provide the criteria for defining a tradition of
    the modern." Sees "certain conditions of twentieth-century
    existence--war, technology and attendant alienation--" as
    major forces shaping the novels examined in this study.

1967

13 SCHOLES, ROBERT. The Fabulators. New York: Oxford
    University Press, pp. 35-46.
        Examines term Black Humor as a modern movement, but also
    as a development in literary history. Finds "the joke is
    one key to the fabulative impulse." Laughter counteracts
    the pain of human existence. Briefly mentions Pynchon as
    one of the writers who have been "stamped with this dark
    label at one time or another."

14 SHRAPNEL, NORMAN. "Excursions Into Strange Worlds."
    Manchester Guardian, 96 (20 April), 11.
        "Exuberant off-beat talent." Oedipus' baffling quest is
    haunting and disquieting. Black Humor with British under-
    currents. This strange writer is a man to watch.

15 SKERRETT, JOSEPH TAYLOR, JR. "Dostoevsky, Nathanael West, and
    Some Contemporary American Fiction." The University of
    Dayton Review, 4, No. 1:23-36.
        Labels Pynchon as one of the Black Humorists--Friedman,
    Heller, Donleavy, Barth and Purdy. Analyzes the common
    characteristics of the Black Humorists. Notes their revival
    of eighteenth century literary customs. V a good example
    because of classical chapter headings and "completely om-
    niscient author." Also "precise effects of language and
    diction." Draws parallels between Nathanael West's four
    novels and the works of the Black Humorists. The absurdity
    of the characters is underlined in V by their names, occu-
    pations, and the counterpointed search of Herbert Stencil
    and Benny Profane. The "unifying common denominator" to
    the thought of the Black Humorists and Nathanael West is
    "a belief in the necessity of living life on a human scale,"
    not in terms of false importances and concepts. Dostoievsky
    heralded the new man, broken in two by the machine age,
    that the Black Humorists portray with good comic irony, not
    Dostoievsky's tragic irony. Good look at an important
    modern movement.

16 SKLAR, ROBERT. "Books and the Arts: The New Novel, U. S. A.:
    Thomas Pynchon." Nation, 205 (25 September), 277-280.
        Ranks Pynchon as "the most intelligent, most audacious
    and most accomplished American novelist writing today."
    Rates The Crying of Lot 49 "a better and more important
    novel than V." Traces themes and images in V and The Cry-
    ing of Lot 49. Sees The Crying of Lot 49 as "a radical po-
    litical novel" that "represents the first step forward for
    American fiction in some time." Good listing of author's
    works.

17 YOUNG, JAMES DEAN. "The Enigma Variations of Thomas Pynchon."
    Critique, 10, No. 1:69-77.
        Suggests V has been misread. Only "superficial likeness
    with the novelists of 'black humor.'" "Life, as Pynchon
    portrays it, is really an enigma." Characterization, his-
    tory and geography are "fictional," but human experience is
    not meaningless; "it is defined partly by speculation and
    partly by experience that one feels should be significant."

                          1968

1   ALDRIDGE, JOHN. "Contemporary Fiction and Mass Culture."
    New Orleans Review, 1:4-9.
        Mentions Pynchon as one of a number of Black Humor
    writers.

2   BYRD, SCOTT. "A Separate War: Camp and Black Humor in Recent
    American Fiction." Language Quarterly, 7 (Fall-Winter),
    7-10.
        Discusses The Crying of Lot 49 in terms of the contra-
    dictory motifs of "camp" and "black humor" in contemporary
    fiction. Compares the ending of the novel with Twain's
    The Mysterious Stranger.

3   ETHRIDGE, JAMES M., BARBARA KOPALA, and CAROLYN RILEY, eds.
    Contemporary Authors: A Bio-Bibliographical Guide to
    Current Authors and Their Works. Vols. 19-20. Detroit:
    Gale Research, pp. 352-354.
        Basic details of Pynchon's life, career, and work. A
    series of short comments on his work by various critics and
    other "sidelights," and a listing of "biographical/critical
    sources."

4   FELDMAN, BURTON. "Anatomy of Black Humor." Dissent,
    15:158-160. Reprinted in The American Novel Since World
    War II.
        Brief mention of Pynchon.

5   FRENCH, MICHAEL R. "The American Novel in the Sixties."
    Midwest Quarterly, 9 (July), 365-379.
        Brief mention of Pynchon.

6   HUNT, JOHN W. "Comic Escape and Anti-Vision: The Novels of
    Joseph Heller and Thomas Pynchon" in Adversity and Grace:
    Studies in Recent American Literature. Edited by Nathan A.
    Scott, Jr. Chicago and London: University of Chicago
    Press, pp. 87-112.

1968

> Pynchon's characters tend to seek avoidance of the in-
> coherences of the modern world in an effort to stabilize
> their environment and keep it within the scope of the pre-
> dictable. This dissociation of the characters from the
> world of their perceptions creates a fundamentally absurd
> position in Pynchon's fiction.

7   KOSTELANETZ, RICHARD. "Dada and the Future of Fiction."
    Works, 1 (Spring), 58-66.
        Briefly mentions Pynchon as one of a number of contempo-
    rary novelists influenced by the Dadaists.

8   McNAMARA, EUGENE. "The Absurd Style in Contemporary American
    Literature." Bulletin de L'Association Canadienne des
    Humanités, 19:44-49.
        Comments on the parallel plots of V: Stencil's search
    for his mother, V, and the story of Benny Profane. The two
    plots interact to disorient the reader by a conflict of fan-
    tasy and reality. The Crying of Lot 49 unites the fantastic
    and the real in the story of Oedipa's quest through a de-
    structive world. Pynchon's second novel may exemplify the
    furthest possibilities of the absurd style.

9   NUMASAWA, KOJI. "Black Humor: An American Aspect." Studies
    in English Literature, 44:177-193.
        Brief mention of Pynchon within a general discussion of
    Black Humor.

10 POIRIER, RICHARD. "The Politics of Self-Parody." Partisan
    Review, 35 (Summer), 339-353.
        Defines literature of self-parody as a newly developed
    form that "makes fun of itself as it goes along." States
    that the "plotting" in V and Lot 49 "has been broadened by
    a Hegelian suspicion that the world itself is governed by
    self-generating political plots and conspiracies more in-
    tricate than any they could devise." Lauds Pynchon for
    giving cults of the sixties the "resonance of a cultural
    tradition." Compares Pynchon with Borge in the invention
    of a new world, the Tristero System. Reprinted in 1971.8.

11 SCHULZ, MAX F. "Pop, Op, and Black Humor: The Aesthetics of
    Anxiety." College English, 30 (December), 230-241.
        Brief comments on Pynchon within a general discussion of
    the relationship between contemporary literature and cul-
    ture.

12   SHAPIRO, STEPHEN. "The Ambivalent Animal: Man in the
       Contemporary British and American Novel." Centennial
       Review, 12:1-22.
             Mentions Pynchon.

                           1969

1   CURLEY, DOROTHY NYREN, MAURICE KRAMER, and ELAINE FIALKA
       KRAMER, eds. A Library of Literary Criticism: Modern
       American Literature. Fourth edition. Vol. 3. New York:
       Frederick Ungar, pp. 35-38.
             Reprints excerpts from seven critical studies of Thomas
       Pynchon's fiction.

2   DAVIS, ROBERT MURRAY. "The Shrinking Garden and New Exits:
       The Comic Satiric Novel in the Twentieth Century." Kansas
       Quarterly, 1:5-16.
             Brief mention of Pynchon.

3   GREENBERG, ALVIN. "The Underground Woman: An Excursion into
       the V-ness of Thomas Pynchon." Chelsea, 27:58-65.
             Explores the contradictory, anti-explanatory nature of
       the conceptual figure of V in Pynchon's novel. Through V,
       Pynchon is able to escape from the embarrassing rationality
       of a falsely ordered world and face the reality of unre-
       mitting chaos.

4   HARTE, BARBARA and CAROLYN RILEY, eds. 200 Contemporary
       Authors: Bio-Bibliographics of Selected Leading Writers of
       Today With Critical and Personal Sidelights.
             Reprinted from Contemporary Authors: A Bio-Bibliographi-
       cal Guide to Current Authors and Their Works. Gale Research
       Co., pp. 223-224.

5   KLEIN, MARCUS, ed. The American Novel Since World War II.
       Greenwich: Fawcet, passim.
             Reprints Burton Feldman's "Anatomy of Black Humor"
       (224-228) and John Barth's "The Literature of Exhaustion"
       (267-279).

6   KOSTELANETZ, RICHARD. "American Fiction of the Sixties."
       In On Contemporary Literature. 2nd edition. New York:
       Avon, pp. 634-652.
             Brief mention of Pynchon.

1969

7   OLDERMAN, RAYMOND MICHAEL. "Beyond the Wasteland: A Study
       of the American Novel in the Nineteen-Sixties." Ph.D.
       Dissertation, Indiana University.
         See 1972.8.

8   POIRIER, RICHARD. "A Literature of Law and Order." Partisan
       Review, 36:189-204.
         The plots of Pynchon's The Crying of Lot 49 and V, the
       intricate and inescapable complexities his characters en-
       counter, "are an expression in Pynchon of the mad belief
       that some plot can ultimately take over the world, can ul-
       timately control life to the point where it is manageably
       inanimate. . . ." Nearly from the outset, the people of
       Pynchon's novels are the instruments of the plots they
       promote." Reprinted in The Performing Self, 1971.8.

9   SCHULZ, MAX F. Radical Sophistication: Studies in
       Contemporary Jewish-American Novelists. Athens: Ohio
       University Press, pp. vii-viii.
         Brief mention of Pynchon.

10   WALDMEIR, JOSEPH J. "Only an Occasional Rutabaga: American
       Fiction Since 1945." Modern Fiction Studies, 15:467-481.
         Brief mention of Pynchon.

11   WASSON, RICHARD. "Notes on a New Sensibility." Partisan
       Review, 36:460-477.
         Discusses Pynchon's rejection of modernism, especially
       the modernist's use of history and myth. Compares Pynchon
       to other twentieth century authors, such as Iris Murdoch
       and D. H. Lawrence.

1970

1   BERGONZI, BERNARD. The Situation of the Novel. Pittsburgh:
       University of Pittsburgh Press, pp. 71-72, 78, 80-83, 87,
       89, 91-93, 96-100, 127, 170, 186, 197.
         Pynchon has been highly influenced by John Barth. Both
       V and The Crying of Lot 49 are intricately plotted, but
       events and characters seldom achieve more fullness than as
       examples of Pynchon's "infinite inventiveness."

2   BRYANT, JERRY H. The Open Decision: The Contemporary American
       Novel and Its Intellectual Background. New York: Free
       Press, pp. 9, 35-36, 40, 249, 252-257.
         Mentions Pynchon.

3   GALLOWAY, DAVID D. The Absurd Hero in American Fiction:
     Updike, Styron, Bellow, Salinger. Austin and London:
     University of Texas Press, p. ix.
         Pynchon avoids the primary problems of an obsession with
     meaninglessness "through his acute comic vision as well as
     sheer stylistic dexterity."

4   GERSTENBERGER, DONNA and GEORGE HENDRICK. "Pynchon, Thomas."
     In The American Novel: A Checklist of Twentieth Century
     Criticism on Novels Written Since 1789. Volume II.
     Criticism Written 1960-1968. Chicago: Swallow, p. 297.
         Lists five unannotated entries of criticism on Pynchon.

5   HALL, JAMES. "The New Pleasures of the Imagination."
     Virginia Quarterly Review, 46 (Autumn), 596-612.
         V is, in part, a novel which reports on the contemporary
     state of the novel as a genre, its relationship with the
     current cultural environment, and the quality of imagina-
     tive fantasy. The "comic fantasy" in Pynchon's novel "cre-
     ates a working model of a world which embraces an ideal of
     spontaneity--and wants to be protected from it."

6   LEARY, LEWIS. Articles on American Literature 1950-1967.
     Durham: Duke University Press, p. 463.
         Lists three unannotated entries of criticism on Pynchon.

7   SAPORTA, MARC. Historie de Roman Americain. Paris: Sighers,
     pp. 281, 282, 290.
         Brief mention of Pynchon.

8   SCOTT, NATHAN A., JR. "The Conscience of the New Literature."
     In The Shaken Realist: Essays in Modern Literature in
     Honor of Frederick J. Hoffman. Edited by Melvin J.
     Friedman and John B. Vickery. Baton Rouge: Louisiana
     State University Press, pp. 251-283.
         Lists Pynchon as one of the novelists of the post-modern
     movement in literature.

9   TANNER, TONY. "The American Novelist as Entropologist."
     London Magazine, n.s. 10 (October), 5-18.
         Pynchon mentioned briefly in a general discussion of
     the "entropologist" motif in contemporary American fiction.

10   WEINBERG, HELEN. The New Novel in America: The Kafkan Mode
     in Contemporary Fiction. Ithaca and London: Cornell
     University Press, pp. 11-12.
         Brief mention of Pynchon.

1971

1 BERTHOFF, WARNER. Fictions and Events: Essays in Criticism
and Literary History. New York: E. P. Dutton, pp. 107,
110, 113.
Brief comments on the theme of conspiracy in The Crying
of Lot 49.

2 HARRIS, CHARLES B. Contemporary American Novelists of the
Absurd. New Haven: Yale University Press, 76–99, passim.
Pynchon's novels are complex extensions of two metaphors
for the situation of contemporary culture: entropy and
quantum theory. These metaphorical relationships of meaning
form the primary thematic structure of The Crying of Lot 49
and V.

3 HAUCK, RICHARD BOYD. A Cheerful Nihilism: Confidence and
"The Absurd" in American Humorous Fiction. Bloomington and
London: Indiana University Press, pp. 11, 237, 242-243.
Brief mention of Pynchon.

4 HENKLE, ROGER B. "Pynchon's Tapestries on the Western Wall."
Modern Fiction Studies, 17 (Summer), 207-220.
Compares Pynchon to Nabokov, discusses the dominant metaphorical patterns in V and The Crying of Lot 49, and the
central theme of proliferation of information and physical
objects beyond the capacity of mental subsumption.

5 KIRBY, DAVID K. "Two Modern Versions of the Quest."
Southern Humanities Review, 5:387-395.
Compares the use of the modern quest motif in the actions
of the governess in Henry James's The Turn of the Screw and
Oedipa Maas in The Crying of Lot 49.

6 LINDBERG-SEYERSTED, BRITA. "American Fiction Since 1950."
Edda, 4:143-203 (201).
Mentions Pynchon as one of the "black humorists" who
"more or less consistently" ridicule accepted and "sacred"
values.

7 MANGEL, ANNE. "Maxwell's Demon, Entropy, Information: The
Crying of Lot 49." Tri-Quarterly, 20:194-208.
Discusses Pynchon's use of thermodynamics, Maxwell's
Demon, entropy and information theory as the conceptual
bases in The Crying of Lot 49. By incorporating an attitude
of unredeemed disorder into his fiction, Pynchon at once es-
capes from the moribund state of modernism and allies his

work with similar contemporary positions found in the other arts.

8   POIRIER, RICHARD. The Performing Self: Compositions and
    Decompositions in the Languages of Contemporary Life.
    New York: Oxford University Press, pp. 10, 14, 18-19,
    23-26, 27-31, 36-38, 42.
        Reprints "A Literature of Law and Order" 1969.8 and "The
    Politics of Self-Parody" 1968.10.

9   SCHOLES, ROBERT. "'Mithridates, he died old': Black Humor
    and Kurt Vonnegut, Jr." In The Sounder Few: Essays from
    the Hollins Critic. Edited by R. H. W. Dillard, George
    Garrett, and John Rees Moore. Athens: University of
    Georgia Press, pp. 173-179.
        Reprints Scholes' article from The Hollins Critic.

10 SCHULZ, MAX F. "The Unconfirmed Thesis: Kurt Vonnegut, Black
    Humor and Contemporary Art." Critique, 12:5-28.
        Comments on V and The Crying of Lot 49 with particular
    attention to the primary Pynchon attitude that "reality" is
    no more than a perceptual construct. Comparisons are drawn
    between Vonnegut, Pynchon, and other contemporary novelists
    and artists.

11 TANNER, TONY. City of Words: American Fiction 1950-1970.
    New York: Harper and Row, pp. 141-180.
        Reprints "The American Novelist as Entropologist" as
    "Everything Running Down" (141-152) and "Caries and Cabals"
    (153-180).

12 _____. "Patterns and Paranoia or Caries and Cabals."
    Salmagundi, 15:78-99.
        Pynchon "writes both to demonstrate the need for fic-
    tions and to impugn or revoke their validity." The open-
    ness of Pynchon's philosophical attitude--for example, the
    centrality of the concept of entropy and the background of
    Henry Adams--is, in some ways, a portrayal of his belief in
    the fictive nature of all explanations, the necessary
    dreams which become fatal illusions.

13 TATHAM, CAMPBELL. "John Barth and the Aesthetics of Artifice."
    Contemporary Literature, 12:60-73.
        Barth, unlike Pynchon, Malamud, Updike, Berger, and the
    Black Humorists, denies the primary engagement with the
    "moral imperative."

<u>1972</u>

1   ABERNATHY, PETER L. "Entropy in Pynchon's <u>The Crying of Lot</u>
    <u>49</u>." <u>Critique</u>, 14:18-33.
    "A central theme of Thomas Pynchon's novel, <u>The Crying</u>
    <u>of Lot 49</u>, is that, because of its entropic tendencies,
    American society has produced a failure in communications
    which leaves its citizens intellectually and spiritually
    dead at the core. Pynchon pictures America as a series of
    closed systems in which the meaning of life . . . is echo-
    ing itself into nothingness." The nature of entropy as
    closed systems is explored with respect to Maxwell's demon,
    the characters of the novel (who "are all presented as
    closed systems"), information, narcissicism, and history.
    <u>The Crying of Lot 49</u> compares to Kesey's <u>One Flew Over the</u>
    <u>Cuckoo's Nest</u> and Farina's <u>Been Down So Long It's Beginning</u>
    <u>to Look Like Up From Here</u>.

2   ANON. "Fiction." <u>Kirkus Reviews</u>, 40 (15 December), 1443.
    Brief review stressing the innovation and difficulty of
    <u>Gravity's Rainbow</u>.

3   DAVIS, ROBERT MURRY. "Parody, Paranoia, and the Dead End of
    Language in <u>The Crying of Lot 49</u>." <u>Genre</u>, 5 (December),
    367-377.
    In <u>The Crying of Lot 49</u>, Pynchon faces the tremendous
    explanatory incoherences in contemporary American culture,
    incoherences subsumed beneath the conflicting possibilities
    of a source of information which can either result in full
    explanation or the complete absence of an explanation. His
    novel "is a particularly good example of the post-realistic
    novel not merely because it uses many of what have become
    stock black comic devices but because it uses them to em-
    body a deeper and ultimately very serious theme, the pos-
    sible death of the American dream or, in broader terms, the
    death of wonder and the total entropy of energy and com-
    munication."

4   GOLDEN, ROBERT E. "Mass Man and Modernism: Violence in
    Pynchon's <u>V</u>." <u>Critique</u>, 14:5-17.
    The primary problem that lies behind and within <u>V</u> is the
    perception of Romantic alienation--the breakdown of cultural
    directions for behavior and the resultant isolation of the
    self. The extension of individual alienation in the twen-
    tieth century leads to the modern mass, a severely hypo-
    statized abstraction, which moves, according to Golden,
    only toward extinction. "In Pynchon humanity is something
    we must learn. The world we live in is our arbitrary

1972

creation; it is we who endow the world with human qualities
and we who either succeed or fail in attaining our humanity
. . . ." Modern man, tired of that guilt and that relentless
intellectual searching which characterize civilization, re-
alizes that his humanity can be abandoned and comes to desire such abandonment."

5 _____. "Violence and Art in Postwar American Literature: A
Study of O'Connor, Kosinski, Hawkes, and Pynchon." Ph.D.
Dissertation, University of Rochester.

6 MAY, JOHN R. Toward a New Earth: Apocalypse in the American
Novel. Notre Dame: Notre Dame University Press,
pp. 172-200.
Views Barth's The End of the Road, Vonnegut's Cat's
Cradle, and Pynchon's The Crying of Lot 49 as exemplifying
the "humorous apocalypse," which May defines as an "imagined
catastrophe that nevertheless provokes laughter." Despite
the humor, The End of the Road and The Crying of Lot 49 give
the sense of lost meaning and a world in disorder.

7 McCONNELL, FRANK. "Pynchon, Thomas." In Contemporary
Novelists. Edited by James Vinson. London: St. James,
pp. 1033-1036.
Discusses the major themes of V and The Crying of Lot 49,
Pynchon's position among contemporary novelists, and his interest in physics. Preceded by a brief summary of biographical facts.

8 OLDERMAN, RAYMOND M. Beyond the Wasteland: A Study of the
American Novel in the Nineteen-Sixties. New Haven: Yale
University Press, pp. 123-149.
Focuses on the imagined and/or real corresponding patterns of meaning invented by the characters in The Crying
of Lot 49 and V. In V, Pynchon sees conspiracy, the center
of meaning and purpose in hidden centralized control,
assumes the nature of possibility.

9 RICHARDSON, ROBERT O. "The Absurd Animate in Thomas Pynchon's
V: A Novel." Studies in the Twentieth Century, 9
(Spring), 35-57.
Discusses the shifting, retreating nature of Pynchon's
characters in V and their relation to the major themes of
the novel. "The novel may provide only 'screwball begin-
nings' for characters who live in a fictive world which is
'breathless and hypomanic,' but Pynchon's treatment of
Fausto and his successors also suggests that the author

119

harbors a preference for the wise which his fascination for
the wised-up does not quite conceal."

10   ROBINSON, DAVID E. "Unaccommodated Man: The Estranged World
      in Contemporary American Fiction." Ph.D. Dissertation,
      Duke University, passim.
           Mentions Pynchon.

11   WEIXLMANN, JOSEPH. "Thomas Pynchon: A Bibliography."
      Critique, 14:34-43.
           This checklist has six sections devoted to different as-
      pects of Pynchon scholarship: "I. Novels and Reviews"
      lists the various editions and reviews of V and The Crying
      of Lot 49. "II. Short Fiction" lists Pynchon's seven
      short stories. "III. Non-Fiction" lists one entry. "IV.
      Biography" lists six sources. "V. Criticism" lists twenty-
      five entries for V, three for The Crying of Lot 49, and
      thirty-seven general studies. "VI. Bibliography" lists
      three entries.

1973

1   ACKROYD, PETER. "Somewhere Over the Novel." Spectator, 231
      (17 November), 641.
           Criticizes the "eccentric ravings" of American critics
      over Gravity's Rainbow as symptomatic of their desire for
      the Great American Novel. The novel's style is "full of
      unnecessary and self-conscious involutions and neologisms,"
      and Pynchon has an uneasy, ironic relationship to his ma-
      terial and the unredeeming character of the novel's ob-
      scenity.

2   ALLEN, BRUCE. "Fiction." Library Journal, 98 (1 March), 766.
           Comments on the highly complex nature of Gravity's Rain-
      bow and Pynchon's style: "the most demanding novel anyone
      has ever written."

3   ANON. Review of Gravity's Rainbow. Publisher's Weekly, 203
      (8 January), 62.
           Describes Gravity's Rainbow as "a Pandora's box of our
      ills." Praises the style and brilliance of the novel.

4   ANON. "The Best and the Brightest." Book World (Washington
      Post), 9 December, p. 1.
           Gravity's Rainbow listed as one of the best books of
      1973.

5   ANON. "Christmas Books." New York Times Book Review,
        2 December, pp. vii, 1.
            Condensed version of Richard Locke's review of Gravity's
        Rainbow.

6   ANON. "Fiction." Booklist, 69 (1 June), 930.
            Brief comment on and plot synopsis of Gravity's Rainbow.

7   ANON. "Language and Literature." Choice, 10 (June), 622.
            Brief review of Gravity's Rainbow, praising Pynchon's
        innovations and the artistic merit of the novel.

8   ANON. "Notes on Current Books." Virginia Quarterly Review,
        49 (Summer), civ.
            Mentions the opacity and paranoia of Gravity's Rainbow.
        Praises Pynchon's extended ability.

9   ANON. "A Selected Vacation Reading List." New York Times
        Book Review, 10 June, pp. vii, 39.
            Brief statement on the theme of Gravity's Rainbow.

10   ANON. "A Selection of the Year's Best Books." Time, 102
        (31 December), 56.
            Gravity's Rainbow is listed.

11   ANON. "Waiting for the Bang." Times Literary Supplement
        (16 November), p. 1389.
            In Gravity's Rainbow, "Mr. Pynchon's marvelous inventive-
        ness is almost entirely without nuance, without resonance:
        the characters, the situations, the words are fixed, comic
        quantities. You may laugh or cry, roll in the aisles or
        leave the cinema--whatever you do, you're still a helpless
        spectator."

12   BELL, PEARL K. "Pynchon's Road of Excess." New Leader, 56
        (2 April), 16-17.
            Gravity's Rainbow is a novel produced by a highly in-
        tellectual and gifted mind, but one that is also in a state
        of "acute disorder." "Pynchon's poetry of chance and high-
        jinks is tedious because it lacks the loving immediacy of
        any sustaining moral vision. When the road of excess leads
        only to another apocalyptic fun-house, it is not worth
        taking."

13   CLEMONS, WALTER. "The Sky's the Limit." Newsweek, 81
        (19 March), 92.
            Brief synopsis of Gravity's Rainbow. The character of
        Slothrop is seen as "too slack of a counterbalance to the
        demonic forces that prevail in the book."

1973

14 COOK, BRUCE. "New Pynchon: Take-Over or Con Job?" <u>National
    Observer</u> (17 March), p. 23.
        Briefly traces Pynchon's career before <u>Gravity's Rainbow</u>
    and the reviewer's ideas on the pseudo-distinction between
    fiction and non-fiction. <u>Gravity's Rainbow</u> turns out to be
    the book which ruins these ideas because it is a "ponderous
    and overblown cartoon of a novel." Pynchon has failed due
    to his "cuteness" and lack of important ideas.

15 DE FEO, RONALD. "Fiction Chronicle." <u>Hudson Review</u>, 26
    (Winter, 1973-74), 773-775.
        Disagrees with the prevalent praise of <u>Gravity's Rainbow</u>
    and the stature of Pynchon. The novel is tedious because
    of its sameness of tone and lack of ideas.

16 GARFITT, ROGER. <u>The Listener</u>, 90 (15 November), 675.
        <u>Gravity's Rainbow</u> does not seem to live up to the praise
    of its American critics. The novel combines the qualities
    of the abstract surreal with the highly sentimental. "It
    works by a principle of spontaneous expansion, whereby the
    mention of any item . . . may suddenly balloon into reveal-
    ing the infrastructure of a global conspiracy."

17 HASSAN, IHAB. <u>Contemporary American Literature: 1945-1972</u>.
    New York: Frederick Ungar, pp. 56, 81, 84-85, 171.
        Pynchon brings the absurd novel to its extreme. His
    purpose: "The obliteration of meaning, the revelation of
    secret yet continuous decay in life <u>and</u> of the patterns
    that inhere even in decay."

18 HILLS, RUST. "Fiction." <u>Esquire</u>, 80 (September), 10, 28.
        Hills put <u>Gravity's Rainbow</u> "into the carton of books
    that are too hard to read and too hard to throw away."

19 KAZIN, ALFRED. <u>The Bright Book of Life: American Novelists
    and Storytellers from Hemingway to Mailer</u>. Boston and
    Toronto: Little, Brown, pp. 275-280.
        History is the "protagonist" of Pynchon's <u>V</u> and <u>The Cry-
    ing of Lot 49</u>. "The key to Pynchon's brilliantly dizzying
    narratives is the force of some hypothesis that is authen-
    tic to him but undisclosable to us."

20 KOLODNY, ANNETTE and DANIEL JAMES PETERS. "Pynchon's <u>The
    Crying of Lot 49</u>: The Novel as Subversive Experience."
    <u>Modern Fiction Studies</u>, 19 (Spring), 79-87.
        The experience of reading <u>The Crying of Lot 49</u> is "sub-
    versive" in that the reader becomes involved in the para-
    noia of the contemporary world and Pynchon's presentation

of it. Pynchon points out the incoherence between language
and behavior in contemporary America and "molds for us a
renewed vision of America expressed in a new language with
new meanings, with the spaces and out of the disillusion-
ment of the old."

21 LEHMAN-HAUPT, CHRISTOPHER. "The Adventures of Rocketman."
    New York Times, 9 March, p. 35.
        Extremely favorable review of Gravity's Rainbow stressing
    the great diversity and innovation of the novel and the
    theme of paranoia. "If I were banished to the moon tomorrow
    and could take only five books along, this would have to be
    one of them. And I suspect that's a feeling that's going
    to last."

22 LEONARD, JOHN. "The Third Law of Reviewer Emotion."
    New York Times Book Review, 10 June, pp. vi, 47.
        Comments on the complexity of Pynchon's fiction--"the
    imaginative equivalent of the Watergate affair."

23 LEVINE, AL. "Paranoia of the Most Grandiose Proportions."
    Commonweal, 98 (4 May), 217-218.
        Gravity's Rainbow is a novel which should be read for
    some of the passages of "seductive" energy, but overall the
    novel is severely flawed by Pynchon's occasional cuteness
    and myopic, paranoid perspective.

24 LEVINE, GEORGE. "V-2." Partisan Review, 40 (Fall), 517-529.
        Pynchon is "the most important American novelist now
    writing." His work is difficult because he "challenges
    fundamental, usually unspoken literary and cultural assump-
    tions." The novel is compared to V and is given a close
    examination in terms of plot, style, and theme. Pynchon's
    position in contemporary literature is positive because he
    challenges us to free ourselves from the "destructive myths
    that support us, and to face, with Pynchon's confidence and
    authority, an irrational world of objects."

25 LHAMON, W. T., JR. "The Most Irresponsible Bastard." New
    Republic, 168 (14 April), 24-28.
        The most important aspect of Gravity's Rainbow is its
    emotional impact. Pynchon constantly surprises the reader
    with a sense of subversion and multiple uncertainties.

26 LINDROTH, J. R. "A Bonus for Fiction Buffs." America, 128
    (12 May), 446.
        Gravity's Rainbow is "an encyclopedia . . . of London
    and Pienemünde experiencing the cataclysm of World War II."

1973

The novel is organized around a quest motif. Pynchon "has
created a watershed for the literary of several decades."

27 LOCKE, RICHARD. "Gravity's Rainbow." New York Times Book
    Review, 11 March, pp. vii, 1-3, 12, 14.
        Speaks of Pynchon in terms of the other major novelists
    of the 1960's, compares his writing to Nabokov and Melville
    (the creation of "Ahabs" and "Ishmaels"), and criticizes
    Gravity's Rainbow for a lack of coherence, fatiguing rest-
    lessness, and the limitations of Pynchon's sensibility.
    "His novel is in this sense a work of paranoid genius, a
    magnificent necropolis that will take its place amidst the
    grand detritus of our culture."

28 LYONS, THOMAS R. and ALLAN D. FRANKLIN. "Thomas Pynchon's
    'Classic' Presentation of the Second Law of Thermodynamics."
    Bulletin of the Rocky Mountain Modern Language Association,
    27:195-204.
        An explanation of Pynchon's use of the Second Law of
    Thermodynamics as a metaphorical basis for the primary
    themes of his fiction, his adherence to the theoretical
    proposition, and his deviation.

29 MADDOCKS, MELVIN. "Paleface Takeover." Atlantic, 231
    (March), 98-100.
        Pynchon is "a theologian . . . laying out the road to
    damnation." Damnation is the major idea of Gravity's
    Rainbow.

30 MENDELSON, EDWARD. "Pynchon's Gravity." Yale Review, 62
    (Summer), 624-631.
        "Pynchon's subject, throughout his work, is not self-
    obsession but the connectedness and coherence of the minute
    particles of the world." Pynchon exemplifies the contem-
    porary world and the attitude that freedom is both necessary
    and possible.

31 MORRIS, ROBERT K. "Jump Off the Golden Gate Bridge." Nation,
    217 (16 July), 53-54.
        The controlling idea of Gravity's Rainbow is that man's
    attempt to create a rationally ordered world is the basic
    root cause of the chaos of the modern world, an idea which
    takes the rocket as "the metaphor of our age and apoca-
    lypse." Pynchon's novel is "a parable of our parabola."

32 MORRISON, PHILIP. "Books." Scientific American, 229
    (October), 131.

The structure of Gravity's Rainbow is a "ballistic para-
bola" linked at its two ends by a V-2 rocket. The intri-
cacies of the novel are formed around metaphors of science
and technology in a wartime situation. Pynchon work is
remarkable.

33 MOYNAHAN, JULIAN. "Misguided Missled." National Observer
      (18 November), p. 39.
      Gravity's Rainbow is not nearly the novel that American
      critics have said it to be. Pynchon's historical sense and
      perception of human interaction are "shallow and juvenile,"
      and his novel is little more than a "pop allegory" of some
      of the more faddish elements of the 1960's.

34 POIRIER, RICHARD. "Rocket Power." Saturday Review of the
      Arts, 1 (March), 59-64.
      It is difficult to classify a novel as "apocalypse" or
      "entropy." More than any other living writer, Pynchon, in
      Gravity's Rainbow, reveals the effects of art and technology
      in modern culture. He shows the Faustian man as a slave to
      the system he thinks he masters. Provides a detailed analy-
      sis of the plot and characters of the novel, particularly
      the central character--the rocket.

35 PRITCHARD, WILLIAM. "Theatre of Operations." New Statesman,
      86 (16 November), 734-735.
      Gravity's Rainbow is "all theatre," which "needs ideally
      to be read aloud." Like The Crying of Lot 49, this novel
      registers "rhetorical urgency," a matter rather sketchily
      examined. Pynchon's inventiveness and alertness make other
      novelists appear simple by comparison.

36 ROSENBAUM, JONATHAN. "One Man's Meat Is Another Man's
      Poison." Village Voice, 29 March, pp. 24, 26.
      "The horror of Pynchon's vision is not merely that we're
      all victims of obsessive plots, but that we're all obsessive
      builders of them." Discusses the immediacy of Pynchon's
      themes and the importance of Slothrop's experiences, es-
      pecially his quest for identity. Gravity's Rainbow is
      Pynchon's most structured and most discursive book.

37 SABRI, M. ARJAMAND. "A Salute to Death." Prairie Schooner,
      47 (Fall), 269-270.
      Gravity's Rainbow is a "giant put-on, an ambitious work
      and an imaginative failure." "Pynchon's text is a negation
      of itself, a celebration of the negative and the void, a
      salute to death." In comparison with the truly great

1973

novels, Gravity's Rainbow lacks the essential quality of human feeling.

38   SCHICKEL, RICHARD. "Paranoia at Full Cry." World, 2
      (10 April), 43-44.
          Examines Pynchon's "paranoid vision of existence."
      Notes the endless range of literary and other references in
      the novel. Gravity's Rainbow is an example of a rampant
      paranoia.

39   SCHULZ, MAX F. Black Humor Fiction of the Sixties. Athens:
      Ohio University Press, pp. 8-9, 61-64, 77-82, 143-145.
          Discusses Pynchon in the context of other novelists of
      the 1960's in terms of character alienation, parody, and
      the historicism of V. Brief mention of Pynchon's "Under
      the Rose."

40   SHEPPARD, R. Z. "V Squared." Time, 101 (5 March), 74-75.
          V is concerned with modern man's desperate attempts to
      construct meaning in a technological world. V is logical
      chaos. The characters are "part of an incomprehensible
      engine whose function is to generate paranoia."

41   SHORRIS, EARL. "The Worldly Palimpsest of Thomas Pynchon."
      Harper's, 246 (June), 78-80, 82.
          Pynchon is a halting, torturous writer who makes reading
      a task. He lacks imagination and all of his novels result
      in criticism and satire--"the art of fiction demands more."
      Comments on V, The Crying of Lot 49, and Gravity's Rainbow.

42   SISSMAN, L. E. "Hieronymus and Robert Bosch: The Art of
      Thomas Pynchon." New Yorker, 49 (19 May), 138-140.
          "Gravity's Rainbow is a picaresque, apocalyptic, absurd-
      ist novel that creates a complex mythology to describe our
      present predicament." Pynchon combines the eye of Hierony-
      mus Bosch in encompassing the strange permutations of con-
      temporary culture and the voice of Robert Bosch--"a German
      magnate of electricity and power"--in the scientific cer-
      tainties of his precise articulations. Pynchon "is almost
      a mathematician of prose, who calculates the least and the
      greatest stress of each word and line, each pun and am-
      biguity, can bear, and applies his knowledge accordingly
      and virtually without lapses, though he takes many scary,
      bracing linguistic risks."

43   THORBURN, DAVID. "A Dissent on Pynchon." Commentary, 55
      (September), 68-70.

Gravity's Rainbow is "brilliant in parts but unfused and exceedingly tedious as a whole." The high praise that the novel has received reveals the uncertain state of our literary culture. The essence of Pynchon's argument is the "absence of freedom." The book fails to portray characters with individuality and "to allow his characters an imaginative space of their own."

44 WOLFF, GEOFFREY. "Gravity's Rainbow." Book World (Washington Post), 11 March, pp. vii, 1-2.
    Gravity's Rainbow defies the possibility for any adequate plot summary since it "trafficks in a bewildering inventory of recondite odds and ends" with which the novel is not really concerned. Pynchon's novel is about "sanity and paranoia, freedom and the social contract, metaphor and truth." Some comments on V and The Crying of Lot 49.

45 WOOD, MICHAEL. "Rocketing to the Apocalypse." New York Review of Books, 20 (22 March), 22-23.
    Gravity's Rainbow is "literally indescribable." As with many modern novels, the setting is the writer's mind. Pynchon's fiction is occasionally stilted, but he is always able to express the difficulty and incomprehensibility of the modern world.

1974

1 ANON. "Books Briefly." Progressive, 38 (February), 66.
    Gravity's Rainbow is a "masterpiece of utterly paranoid fiction."

2 ANON. "Paperbacks." National Observer (3 November), p. 29.
    Comments briefly on the plot of The Crying of Lot 49 (Penguin edition).

3 ANON. "Paperbacks of the Month." New York Times Book Review, 10 March, pp. vii, 28, 30.
    Brief review of Gravity's Rainbow (Bantam). Describes the setting of the novel and earlier comments on the novel in the New York Times Book Review.

4 COLE, WILLIAM. "Tradewinds." Saturday Review/World, 1 (7 February), 42.
    Brief mention of Gravity's Rainbow as "the greatest novel I never finished and [which] will win the National Book Award."

Writings about Thomas Pynchon, 1963-1975

1974

5   DOHERTY, PAUL C. "The Year's Best in Paperbacks." _America_,
    130 (9 February), 94.
        The formidable difficulties of _Gravity's Rainbow_ make
    demands upon the reader like those of no other novel. Pyn-
    chon's novel is about "our unconscious drives for authen-
    ticity" and "how hopeless they are."

6   JORDAN, CLIVE. "World Enough, and Time." _Encounter_, 42
    (February), 62-64.
        Stresses the range of allusions and verbal manipulations
    in _Gravity's Rainbow_, but criticizes Pynchon for insuffi-
    cient sympathy with his characters.

7   KIHSS, PETER. "Pulitzer Jurors Dismayed on Pynchon."
    New York Times, 8 May, p. 38.
        Concerns the rejection of Pynchon and _Gravity's Rainbow_
    for the Pulitzer Prize.

8   LELAND, JOHN P. "Pynchon's Linguistic Demon: _The Crying of
    Lot 49_." _Critique_, 16:45-53.
        Deals with the fictive nature of language and the lack
    of congruency between language and the phenomenal world.
    The reader of _The Crying of Lot 49_ experiences an informa-
    tion overload in the absence of explanatory categories that
    might allow him to explain the "meaning" of the novel--the
    same type of information overload experienced by Oedipa
    Maas in her search for the meaning of the Tristero System
    and Iverarity's past.

9   LIPSIUS, FRANK. "The American Lit Fit." _Books and Bookmen_,
    19 (March), 64-66 (65-66).
        Mentions Pynchon as a new kind of tale-spinner and de-
    scribes _Gravity's Rainbow_ as a book which, "despite the
    richness of images and plethora of events," moves "in a
    chilling back street of vapid sterility."

10 McLELLAN, JOSEPH. "Paperbacks." _Book World_ (_Washington Post_),
    7 April, p. 4.
        Brief comments on _Gravity's Rainbow_ (Bantam edition).

11 OZIER, LANCE. "Antipointsman/Antimexico: Some Mathematical
    Imagery in _Gravity's Rainbow_." _Critique_, 16:73-90.
        Gravity's Rainbow is the first instance where Pynchon
    uses scientific and mathematical allusions and metaphors to
    substantially enhance his depth of characterization and
    theme. Pointsman and Mexico are used as examples of Pyn-
    chon's use of mathematical metaphors to differentiate be-
    tween the characters--"the idea of a probablistic model and

the associated concept of points on the number line between
and including zero and one." The range of associations in
Gravity's Rainbow that extend from this metaphor move into
the major forms of the theoretical concern and submission
to non-causal unpredictability, a situation where fictive
categories of subsumption are created to allow the individual to function.

12 PATTESON, RICHARD. "What Stencil Knew: Structure and
    Certitude in Pynchon's V." Critique, 16:30-44.
        V presents various explanations of meaning which are
    constantly being established and then undermined, so that
    the experience of the reader parallels the experience of
    Stencil. Explanations are only fictive illusions of per-
    manence--the paradox of knowledge resulting only in knowing
    that certainty is irrelevant.

13 RILEY, CAROLYN and BARBARA HART, eds. Contemporary Literary
    Criticism: Excerpts from Criticism of the Works of Today's
    Novelists, Poets, Playwrights, and Other Creative Writers.
    Vol. II. Detroit: Gale Research, pp. 408-420.
        Reprints sixteen excerpts from Pynchon criticism.

14 RUSSELL, CHARLES. "The Vault of Language: Self-Reflective
    Artifice in Contemporary American Fiction." Modern Fiction
    Studies, 20 (Autumn), 349-359.
        Pynchon's novels, particularly V, evolve patterns in
    which the characters attempt to mask the inevitable fact of
    silence (and the unstated "desire for a state of inanimate-
    ness") by constructing linguistic, illusory explanations--
    historical explanations. Compares Pynchon to Barthelme,
    Kosinski, Barth, Brautigan, and Sukenick.

15 SIMMON, SCOTT. "A Character Index: Gravity's Rainbow."
    Critique, 16:68-72.
        A character finding list for Gravity's Rainbow. Entry
    page numbers are keyed to the Viking/Compass edition.

16 _____. "Gravity's Rainbow Described." Critique, 16:54-67.
        Examines the four primary subplots and the major groups
    of characters in Gravity's Rainbow. Comments on Pynchon's
    exploitation of cinematic form in which a dualistic vision
    and a continuous structure combine. Gravity's Rainbow
    transmutes the waste and contradictions of contemporary
    culture "into a rainbow," an overview that unifies the
    discontinuities.

1974

17 SLADE, JOSEPH W. Thomas Pynchon. Foreword by Terence Malley.
    New York: Warner.
        This is an introduction to Pynchon's works for the
    general reader. Slade begins with a discussion of Pynchon's
    short stories and "A Journey Into the Mind of Watts." Two
    chapters on V, one on The Crying of Lot 49, and two chap-
    ters on Gravity's Rainbow follow. The final chapter,
    "Garbage Dumps and Genius," brings together various strains
    of Pynchon's intellectual interests and places him within
    the context of other contemporary novelists. The primary
    concern in this study is Pynchon's ideas and how they both
    reflect, refract, and analyze the nature of contemporary
    culture and some of the primary modes of contemporary in-
    tellectual thought.

18 STICKNEY, JOHN. "A Reader's Guide to Thomas Pynchon."
    Mademoiselle, 80 (December), 27, 38.
        Discusses the mysterious, enigmatic personality of Pyn-
    chon and the major qualities of The Crying of Lot 49, V,
    and Gravity's Rainbow: the concern with mechanization, the
    quest, stylistic discontinuity, apocalyptic vision, punning
    humor, and "ominous logic."

                            1975

1   HENDIN, JOSEPHINE. "What Is Thomas Pynchon Telling Us?"
    Harper's, 250 (March), 82-92.
        In his first novel, Pynchon explored the reciprocal
    dilemma of destructiveness and vulnerability through caring
    and presented characters who emerge as disengaged and un-
    feeling. The only way out "is to deadlock the two" aspects
    "in endless, profane life, forever content." Here, what-
    ever is order becomes disorder through the irresistable
    entropy. "Pynchon went still further in affirming limita-
    tion as the sole purpose of existence. Given our destruc-
    tiveness . . . our mission on earth, Pynchon concludes,
    must be to elevate the devil. 'Our mission is to promote
    death.'" Compares Gravity's Rainbow with The Magic Mountain
    and Ulysses.

2   HERZBERG, BRUCE. "Selected Articles on Thomas Pynchon: An
    Annotated Bibliography." Twentieth Century Literature, 21
    (May), 221-225.
        An annotated checklist of critical studies of Pynchon's
    work and reviews of V, The Crying of Lot 49, and Gravity's
    Rainbow.

                            130

1975

3 LE CLAIR, THOMAS. "Death and Black Humor." Critique,
   17:5-40.
       Discusses the apocalyptic nature of death and the dual
   nature of death and eroticism in Pynchon's novels.

4 LHAMON, W. T., JR. "Pentacost, Promiscuity, and Pynchon's V:
   From the Scaffold to the Impulsive." Twentieth Century
   Literature, 21 (May), 163-176.
       Concerns the basic paradoxical relationships in V with
   some remarks on Pynchon's other works and the shift from
   modernist to postmodernist ideologies.

5 OZIER, LANCE W. "The Calculus of Transformation: More
   Mathematical Imagery in Gravity's Rainbow." Twentieth
   Century Literature, 21 (May), 193-210.
       Details a number of mathematical allusions in Gravity's
   Rainbow. These allusions and the patterns of recurrence
   that Pynchon allows form the basic unity of the novel.

6 POIRIER, RICHARD. "The Importance of Thomas Pynchon."
   Twentieth Century Literature, 21 (May), 151-162.
       Discusses the innovations in Pynchon's fiction, the
   likely possibility of the destruction of his works by the
   academic reader (in the same way that Joyce and Eliot have
   been destroyed), and the essence of Pynchon's fiction in
   the "cultural inundation" of the works and the experience
   of random behavior and information.

7 RILEY, CAROLYN, ed. Contemporary Literary Criticism:
   Excerpts from Criticism of the Works of Today's Novelists,
   Poets, Playwrights, and Other Creative Writers. Vol. III.
   Detroit: Gale Research, pp. 408-420.
       Reprints excerpts from thirteen critical reviews and
   articles on Pynchon.

8 SANDERS, SCOTT. "Pynchon's Paranoid History." Twentieth
   Century Literature, 21 (May), 177-192.
       Concentrates on Gravity's Rainbow. "My purpose . . . is
   to show how this conspiratorial view of history [as defined
   by Richard Hofstadter in The Paranoid Style in American
   Politics and Other Essays] structures Pynchon's fiction, to
   examine some of its stylistic consequences, and to elaborate
   the suggestion . . . that it is rooted in a theology from
   which God has been withdrawn."

9 SCHMITZ, NEIL. "Describing the Demon: The Appeal of Thomas
   Pynchon." Partisan Review, 42:112-125.

1975

> In Pynchon's fiction and particularly in Gravity's Rainbow, the idea of a deterministic historical process is abandoned. This historical perspective "has no destination, no implicit meaning—it is only a place, an environment, a theater."

10   VESTERMAN, WILLIAM. "Pynchon's Poetry." Twentieth Century Literature, 21 (May), 211-220.
Examines the thematic and stylistic purposes of the poetry inclusions in Pynchon's three novels.

11   WINSTON, MATTHEW. "The Quest for Pynchon." Twentieth Century Literature, 21 (October), 278-287.
Brings together a number of biographical fragments about Pynchon and is the clearest and most detailed exploration of Pynchon's self-imposed anonymity.

Index

This Index is intended to provide access to the information on Barth, Kosinski, and Pynchon contained in the sections listing works about these writers. There are three separate parts of the Index, one each on Barth, Kosinski, and Pynchon. These give the location of items by particular authors who have written about Barth, Kosinski, and Pynchon, and all of the entries in the bibliographies that specifically deal with their individual works. The listing for each entry is followed by a notation of where the work can be found. Thus, the first entry in the Barth Index reads:

Adams, P., 1968.1; 1972.1

Translation: In the section devoted to writings about John Barth, under the year 1968, P. Adams' work on Barth will be the first entry listed.

Index to John Barth

Adams, P., 1968.1; 1972.1
Adelman, G., 1956.1
Allen, B., 1972.2
Alter, R., 1966.1
Altieri, C., 1971.1
Anon., 1956.2, 3; 1957.1;
    1958.1-3; 1960.1-3; 1961.1;
    1963.1, 2; 1965.1, 2;
    1966.2-9; 1967.1-8; 1968.2-4;
    1969.1-3; 1972.3-8; 1973.1, 2
Appel, A., Jr., 1968.5
Ardery, P., 1968.6
Axthelm, P., 1968.7

Bailey, P., 1969.4
Balliett, W., 1966.10
Bannon, B., 1966.11
Barker, S., 1960.4
Beagle, P. S., 1966.12
Bean, J., 1971.2
Bellamy, J. D., 1972.9, 10
Bienstock, B., 1973.3
Bluestone, G., 1960.5
Boyers, R., 1968.8
Bradbury, J., 1969.5
Bradbury, M., 1962.3
Breslin, J., 1972.11
Bryant, J., 1970.1; 1972.12
Bryer, J., 1963.1
Burgess, A., 1967.9
Byrd, S., 1966.13; 1968.9

Chimera, 1972.1-8, 11-14, 16, 18,
    20, 21, 23, 25; 1973.1, 2, 4,
    6, 12
Churchill, T., 1971.3
Coleman, J., 1962.4
Cooper, M., 1956.4

Corbett, E., 1966.14
Corke, H., 1967.10
Crinklew, W., 1972.13

Davenport, G., 1968.10
Davis, D., 1966.15; 1968.11
Dippie, B., 1969.6
Diser, P., 1968.12
Donoghue, D., 1966.16

Elliott, G., 1968.13
Ellmann, M., 1973.4
Enck, J., 1965.3
End of the Road, The, 1958.1-5;
    1959.1; 1960.1, 5, 7, 11;
    1962.1-4, 6-8; 1963.4, 5;
    1965.3-5, 9, 10; 1966.8, 12,
    15-21, 24, 26, 32, 33, 36,
    39; 1967.6, 23; 1968.4, 6, 8,
    11, 13, 16, 18, 29, 33;
    1969.9, 10, 14, 19; 1970.1,
    4, 6, 11; 1971.6-8, 12, 14;
    1972.9, 12, 15, 17, 23, 24;
    1973.3, 5, 6, 9-11
Ethridge, J., 1962.5
Ewell, B., S.S.N.D., 1973.5

Featherstone, J., 1966.17
Fenton, J., 1969.7
Fiedler, L., 1960.6; 1964.1;
    1968.14; 1969.8; 1971.4
Floating Opera, The, 1956.1-13;
    1957.1; 1958.3; 1959.1;
    1960.5-7; 1963.2-5; 1965.3-5,
    9, 10; 1966.8, 12, 15-21, 26,
    32, 33, 36, 39; 1967.1, 2, 6,
    11, 22, 23; 1968.4-6, 11,
    17-19, 27, 28; 1969.15;

135

1970.1, 4-6; 1971.6-8, 10,
14, 15; 1972.8, 9, 12, 24,
25; 1973.3, 5, 6, 10
Fremont-Smith, E., 1966.18;
1968.15
Fuller, E., 1960.7

Garis, R., 1966.19; 1969.9
Giles Goat-Boy, 1965.3;
1966.2-22, 24-31, 33, 34,
36-38, 40-42; 1967.1-4, 6-10,
12-21, 23; 1968.2-6, 9-11,
13, 18-21, 27, 31, 32, 34;
1969.1, 4, 7-10, 14, 16;
1970.1-5, 9, 10; 1971.3,
5-8, 11, 14, 15; 1972.4, 9,
12, 16, 19, 22, 24, 25;
1973.3, 4, 6, 10
Golwyn, J., 1956.5
Graff, G., 1968.16
Graham, K., 1968.17
Gross, B., 1968.18

Haney, F., 1967.11
Harding, W., 1956.6, 7; 1960.8;
1966.20; 1968.19
Harper, H., Jr., 1971.5
Harris, C. B., 1971.6
Harvey, D., 1969.10
Hassan, I., 1962.6
Hauck, R., 1970.2; 1971.7
Hendin, J., 1973.6
Hicks, G., 1965.4; 1966.21;
1968.20, 21; 1970.3
Hill, H., 1968.22
Hill, W., S.J., 1966.22; 1968.23
Hilliam, B., S.J., 1972.14
Hinden, M., 1973.7
Hirsh, D., 1972.15
Hjortsberg, W., 1969.11
Hogan, W., 1956.8
Holder, A., 1968.24
Hood, S., 1969.12
Hyman, S. E., 1965.5; 1966.23

Johnson, B., 1967.12
Jones, D., 1973.8
Joseph, G., 1970.4

Kazin, A., 1973.9
Kenedy, R., 1971.8

Kennard, J., 1970.5
Kerner, D., 1959.1
Kiely, B., 1966.24
King, F., 1961.2
Kitching, J., 1966.25
Klein, M., 1966.26
Kostelanetz, R., 1965.6, 7;
1967.13

Lahaye, J., 1958.4
Lebowitz, N., 1971.9
Le Clair, T., 1973.10
Lee, L., 1968.25
Leff, L., 1971.10
Lehmann-Haupt, 1972.16
Lemon, L., 1969.13
Levine, P., 1967.14
Lifson, H., 1967.15
Lodge, D., 1967.16
Lost in the Funhouse, 1968.1-3,
5-7, 10, 11, 15, 19-21, 23,
26, 30, 31; 1969.1, 3, 4, 7,
9, 11-14, 17, 18; 1970.4, 7;
1971.1, 5, 7, 14; 1972.4, 8,
16; 1973.3, 6, 7

McCohn, P., 1966.27
McGuiness, F., 1967.17
McLaughlin, R., 1960.9
MacNamara, D., 1967.18
Majdiak, D., 1970.6
Malin, I., 1966.28, 29
Mandel, S., 1956.9
May, J. R., 1972.17
Meras, P., 1966.30
Mercer, P., 1971.11
Meyer, A., 1973.11
Michaels, L., 1972.18
Morse, J. M., 1966.31
Murray, J., 1968.26
Myers, A., 1956.10

Noland, R., 1966.32

O'Connell, S., 1966.33
Olderman, R., 1972.19

Paulson, R., 1971.12
Perkins, B., 1972.20
Petersen, C., 1967.19

Index to Jerzy Kosinski

Index to Thomas Pynchon

Hendin, J., 1975.1
Hendrick, G., 1970.4
Henkle, R. B., 1971.4
Herzberg, B., 1975.2
Hicks, G., 1966.15
Hills, R., 1973.18
Hoffman, F. J., 1963.14
Hunt, J. W., 1968.6
Hyman, S. E., 1963.15; 1964.4;
   1966.16, 17

Jordan, C., 1974.6
"Journey Into the Mind of Watts,
   A," 1972.11

Kazin, A., 1973.19
Kihss, P., 1974.7
Kirby, D. K., 1971.5
Klein, M., 1969.5
Koch, S., 1964.5
Kolodny, A., 1973.20
Kostelanetz, R., 1965.5-7;
   1968.7; 1969.6

Larner, J., 1963.16
Leary, L., 1970.6
Le Clair, T., 1975.3
Lehan, R., 1967.9
Lehman-Haupt, C., 1973.21
Leland, J. P., 1974.8
Leonard, J., 1973.22
Levine, A., 1973.23
Levine, G., 1973.24
Levine, P., 1963.17
Lewis, R. W. B., 1965.8
Lhamon, W. T., Jr., 1973.25;
   1975.4
Lindberg-Seyersted, B., 1971.6
Lindroth, J. R., 1973.26
Lipsius, F., 1974.9
Locke, R., 1973.27
"Low-Lands," 1972.11
Lyons, T. R., 1973.28

McConnell, F., 1972.7
McLellan, J., 1974.10
McNamara, E., 1968.8
Maddocks, M., 1973.29
Malkin, M. A., 1966.19
Mangel, A., 1971.7
May, J. R., 1972.6

Meixner, J. A., 1963.18
Mendelson, E., 1973.30
Miller, J. E., Jr., 1967.10
Morris, R. K., 1973.31
Morrison, P., 1973.32
"Mortality and Mercy in Vienna,"
   1972.11
Moynahan, J., 1973.33

Nelson, M. E., Jr., 1966.20
Nichols, L., 1963.19
Numasawa, K., 1968.9

Olderman, R. M., 1969.7; 1972.8
Ozier, L., 1974.11; 1975.5

Patteson, R., 1974.12
Petersen, C., 1965.9
Phillips, W., 1965.10
Plimpton, G., 1963.20
Poirier, R., 1963.21; 1966.21,
   22; 1968.10; 1969.8; 1971.8;
   1973.34; 1975.6
Pollack, V., 1963.22
Price, R. G. G., 1967.11
Pritchard, W., 1973.35

Richardson, A. O., 1972.9
Ricks, C., 1963.23
Riley, C., 1974.13; 1975.7
Ritter, J. P., Jr., 1967.12
Robinson, D. E., 1972.10
Rose, R., 1966.23
Rosenbaum, J., 1973.36
Rosenthal, R., 1966.24
Ross, A., 1963.24
Russell, C., 1974.14

Sabri, M. A., 1973.37
Sanders, S., 1975.8
Saporta, M., 1970.7
Schickel, R., 1973.38
Schmitz, N., 1975.9
Scholes, R., 1967.13; 1971.9
Schulz, M. F., 1968.11; 1969.9;
   1971.10; 1973.39
Scott, N. A., Jr., 1970.8
"Secret Integration, The,"
   1972.11
Shapiro, S., 1968.12
Shattuck, R., 1966.25

Sheppard, R. Z., 1973.40
Shorris, E., 1973.41
Shrapnel, N., 1967.14
"Shrink Flips, The," 1972.11
Simmon, S., 1974.15, 16
Sissman, L. E., 1973.42
Skerrett, J. T., Jr., 1967.15
Sklar, R., 1967.16
Slade, J. W., 1974.17
Slatoff, W., 1963.25
Stikney, J., 1974.18

Tanner, T., 1970.9; 1971.11, 12
Tatham, C., 1971.13
Thorburn, D., 1973.43
Trachtenberg, S., 1966.26

"Under the Rose," 1972.11

V, 1963.1-26; 1964.1-5; 1965.1-10;
    1966.5, 9, 13, 14, 16-18, 20,
    25; 1967.2, 10, 12-17;

1968.1, 3-12; 1969.1-11;
    1970.1-10; 1971.2-4, 6, 9-13;
    1972.4-11; 1973.17, 19, 24,
    28, 39-41, 44; 1974.12-14,
    17-18; 1975.1-4, 6, 7, 10, 11
Vesterman, W., 1975.10

Waldmeir, J. J., 1969.10
Wasson, R., 1969.11
Weinberg, H., 1970.10
Weixlmann, J., 1972.11
Wensberg, E., 1966.27
Winston, M., 1975.11
Wolff, G., 1973.44
Wood, M., 1973.45
Wood, P., 1963.26
"World (This One), The Flesh
    (Mrs. Oedipa Maas), and the
    Testament of Pierce Inverar-
    ity, The," 1972.11

Young, J. D., 1967.17